Praise for
Bring Your Human to Work

"This is an important moment. We are all trying to figure out how to create a workplace that's inclusive, meaningful, and inspires the kind of creativity that leads to innovation. Erica Keswin's heartfelt, accessible, well-researched book, *Bring Your Human to Work*, is what we've all been waiting for."

—KATIE COURIC
journalist and bestselling author

"When people thrive, business thrives. And that's why companies that prioritize employee well-being will win the future. In *Bring Your Human to Work*, Erica Keswin shares the science and the stories of companies that get it right. If you want to build a thriving workforce, this book is for you."

—ARIANNA HUFFINGTON
founder of Huffington Post and
founder and CEO of Thrive Global

"If you care about people as much as profits, this book is full of useful ideas for making work life better."

—ADAM GRANT
New York Times bestselling author of *Give and Take*,
Originals, and *Option B* with Sheryl Sandberg

"One of the best employee habits is honoring relationships—with colleagues, clients, and ourselves. Erica Keswin shares the science and stories from companies about how great relationships happen."

—CHARLES DUHIGG
bestselling author of *The Power of Habit*
and *Smarter Faster Better*

"In her impactful new book, Erica Keswin digs deep through relatable, real-world examples to uncover how working human is essential to both honoring relationships and helping employees feel happier and more fulfilled in the work they do each day. She also uncovers a universal truth that affects all of us: recognition is a fundamental human need, one that can influence everything we do. Her book is aptly named; it's time for us all to bring our human to work."

—DEREK IRVINE
vice president, client strategy and
consulting at Globoforce

"In a world where busy is equated with status, competence and ambition, people are seemingly having a more and more difficult time disconnecting. And in our quest for busy we have lost our, as Keswin says, 'Human!' In *Bring Your Human to Work*, she discusses practical strategies for building workplace cultures that embrace our human, using technology as a tool for good, and helping us form more meaningful connections. If we are to build a more human workplace, this is a book not to be missed!"

—GAIL BERGER, PhD
assistant professor of instruction in industrial
engineering and management sciences at Northwestern
University, Kellogg School of Management

"This book gives the reader a rich collection of actionable steps which any organization can use to become more authentic, genuine, and human. It is chock-full of examples from large and small firms, high-tech and no-tech organizations, start-ups and established companies. I guarantee you'll come away with good ideas for making the firm you work in even more human."

— JACK ZENGER
bestselling author and CEO of Zenger-Folkman,
a firm dedicated to elevating leadership behavior

"This insightful book is loaded with action plans, resources, powerful statistics, and real-life stories of heart-centered leaders and their organizations. If you are looking for an actionable list of things to do to up-level your culture and bring more human to work, *Bring Your Human to Work* is a lovely guide offering us easy-to-integrate steps and practices to bring our human in."

—ANESE CAVANAUGH
author of *Contagious Culture*,
and creator of the IEP Method®

"Erica Keswin's *Bring Your Human to Work* will transform the way you think about finding meaning and connection through your work. It is a must-read for anyone passionate about building a purpose-driven life and career. There are so many essential lessons for business and nonprofit leaders on how to build a culture that inspires the very best from their people."

—SHIZA SHAHID
cofounder of Malala Fund, and founder of NOW Ventures

"*Bring Your Human to Work* highlights an important message and one that I've always believed: building relationships is one of the most important aspects in building any business. This is more important than ever in our digital age. Read this book, invest in relationships. Your business will thank you."

—SHELLEY ZALIS
CEO of the Female Quotient, and founder
of the Girls' Lounge

*Matt,
keep bringing
your human to
work! Best* EK

Bring Your

HUMAN

to Work

10 Surefire Ways to Design a Workplace That's Good for
People, Great for Business, and Just Might Change the World

Erica Keswin

Mc
Graw
Hill
Education

New York Chicago San Francisco Athens London Madrid
Mexico City Milan New Delhi Singapore Sydney Toronto

1 2 3 4 5 6 7 8 9 LCR 23 22 21 20 19 18

ISBN   978-1-260-11809-4
MHID   1-260-11809-6

e-ISBN   978-1-260-11810-0
e-MHID   1-260-11810-X

Library of Congress Cataloging-in-Publication Data

Names: Keswin, Erica, author.
Title: Bring your human to work : 10 surefire ways to design a workplace that is good for people, great for business, and just might change the world / Erica Keswin.
Description: New York : McGraw-Hill, [2019] | Includes bibliographical references.
Identifiers: LCCN 2018018927| ISBN 9781260118094 (alk. paper) | ISBN 1260118096
Subjects: LCSH: Corporate culture. | Organizational behavior. | Employee motivation. | Quality of work life. | Social responsibility of business.
Classification: LCC HD58.7 .K464565 2019 | DDC 658.3/12--dc23 LC record available at https://lccn.loc.gov/2018018927

McGraw-Hill Education products are available at special quantity discounts to use as premiums and sales promotions or for use in corporate training programs. To contact a representative, please visit the Contact Us pages at www.mhprofessional.com.

This book is dedicated to my husband, Jeff, and our three little humans, Julia, Caroline, and Daniel.

CONTENTS

INTRODUCTION

Getting Started on This Human Business

I've always been a connector. Whether I was connecting people with great jobs as an executive recruiter, or setting up marriages as a side hustle, I've long believed in the importance of connection. I also know firsthand that, in this digital age, it's getting harder and harder to set aside our devices and the alluring promise of all those digital "friends." Even for me.

Which is to say I get why my three teenage kids feel so drawn to their digital lives. I understand how digital distractions complicate the workplace. I see the challenges, because technology is front and center in all of our lives.

I remember a lunch with a close friend where technology completely changed the dynamic of our friendship. My girlfriend couldn't put away her phone when I tried to confide in her. Every time I opened my mouth to share something, she would look down, or her phone would buzz again and again, until I finally gave up.

In my role as a workplace strategist for the past 25 years, my focus has been on helping companies improve their performance through people. A few years ago, I started seeing behaviors I had not seen before. More and more, employees were calling into meetings from down the hall, texting bad news to clients instead of calling, and eating lunch alone at their desks, wearing headphones.

Parents, friends, CEOs, and managers all know that something's off, but they don't know exactly what it is, or how to fix it.

Let's face it. We're living in the Wild West. And there's no new sheriff coming to town.

That's one of the reasons why I wrote this book—to help create some rules of the road. At home, at school, and in the workplace, we're frowning into our phones, shooting for "Inbox Zero," and obsessively framing our lives into selfie-ops instead of living them. In so many ways, we're missing out on one another.

I wrote *Bring Your Human to Work* to inspire and guide those of us who want to be truly connected, to be real humans— in our lives, and especially at work.

What It Means to Be Human

Over the last five years, I started hearing a buzz about "human" workplaces. Even the most senior leaders—male ones at that— were talking about being vulnerable, compassionate, and yes, human. I found myself wondering: "What did people mean by 'working human'?" "As opposed to what?" I wanted to know.

What I've discovered is that while everyone uses the term "human" differently, they are all pointing in the same general direction: people crave work-life balance, sustainable work practices, and authentic, purpose-driven work cultures. People are no longer willing to accept work as a soul-crushing, Dilbertesque, cubicled nightmare. However, as with many trends, while a strong, shared sentiment is being expressed and a legitimate problem is being revealed, the solutions are a little bit all over the place. I became very curious about this so-called "human" business, and I wanted to learn more. I set out to investigate the buzz and to determine if it really matters.

After talking to hundreds of CEOs, entrepreneurs, managers, and employees around the country, I have found that, in light of the digital deluge occurring around us, we all need a more human workplace. Putting phones in a basket during a meeting, eliminating email, ensuring that employees take vacation—all of these mini-fixes are on the right track. But I've learned that there is one thing anyone and everyone can do to ensure a more human workplace: *Honor relationships.*

A human workplace honors relationships. And yes, it matters.

Bringing your human to work is not rocket science, but that doesn't mean it's easy. It takes hard work and discipline. It requires honoring relationships in everything we do—creating our values, running meetings, deciding who we hire, using technology, choosing whom we partner with, and evaluating and rewarding talent. Working human in the twenty-first century means that we absolutely must come to terms with the ubiquitous digital presence that sometimes feels overwhelming but can also be a powerful tool for getting ourselves, our products, and our messages out there. Bringing our human to work is both about putting technology in its place in order to build strong relationships and about inviting technology to the table, making good use of everything that can create a more human workplace.

Bringing our human to work will help us manage our technology and ourselves, too. Yet that's not the only reason this book is so important for businesses today. As you may have heard, the millennial generation (people born between 1981 and 1996) will comprise nearly 75 percent of the global work-force by 2025.[1] These young, passionate people are changing the game in many important ways. And their influence on today's society and workplace includes a demand for a more human life at work.

For instance, this generation has redefined what it means to be "social," blurring the boundaries between private, pub-lic, and work lives, and demanding that company values be taken off the walls and actually felt through the halls. Millen-nials want their work lives to have meaning and to work for companies that lead with a purposeful culture. Too many busi-ness owners aren't sure how to do that or even what it means. I know, though, that meaningful values play an important role in the human workplace.

So for starters, let's define "culture." Culture refers to how it *feels* to interact with a company, as a consumer, an employee, a vendor, or a partner. What is the company vibe or personality? How do people behave when nobody's looking? Culture is important, often thought to be number one on the list of critical factors in building a successful business. One of my favorite companies is JetBlue, a true leader in establishing a human workplace (and a company I have studied in depth). They hold top leaders accountable for maintaining the super cool, connected feeling of their corporate culture. Management is expected to show up to flip burgers at the holiday barbeque, attend regular new-hire orientations, and uphold and promote this uncommonly human culture. They are evaluated on how well they do this—in fact, their bonuses are based on it!

So let's agree that culture matters. But what *kind* of culture is a human culture? Fun cultures are great. By-any-means-necessary money-making cultures certainly have their fans. A *meaningful* culture—a place where people can feel like they are plugged into something bigger than themselves—that's a human culture. That's the kind of place that businesses need to create if they want to succeed in this purpose-driven marketplace and the race for young, very-much-in-demand talent.

As important as culture is, it is just one part of creating a human workplace. Honoring relationships is the theme that brings everything a human workplace stands for together. What does this mean, on the ground, in your particular company? And even if you get it right, will all this human business help the bottom line?

Here's a number to consider: $300 billion. According to the American Institute of Stress, $300 billion is lost in our economy every year to stress.[2] Imagine the human impact we could make if we could get that money back. Or, better yet, if that stress hadn't happened in the first place. By working human, I believe we can begin to literally cut our losses and cultivate a more human world.

Prepare to change the way you do business.

How This Book Is Structured: Picking and Choosing from a Menu of Human Options

A human business, like a human being, is both incredibly complex and utterly simple. Our basic needs are few (food, water, shelter, affection), but the ways we go about meeting those needs are infinite. Let's say you've established that you want to bring your human to work. Great! *Sign me up!* But, what's next?

Maybe you've heard about B Corps, those for-profit companies that are certified as being "of benefit" to the world, and maybe you think you should convert your business into one that gives something away for each sale, like they do at Toms or

Warby Parker. What if you are a marketing agency? An architect? A management consultant? How would you do that?

Should you develop an entire language like JetBlue's, where employees drink what they call the "Blue Juice," the brand-specific language that makes them who they are? Should you create a values-alignment position, like Etsy; a chief purpose officer, like PwC; or a chief culture officer, like Union Square Hospitality Group?

Maybe you're wondering: Is texting with clients okay? How can we get the most out of our meetings? What does it mean to actually be "present"? What's the deal with vacations? If vacations are unlimited, why are people not taking them? How do you manage your emails so you have time to connect with your team? Are performance reviews a human way to evaluate employees? What kind of space works best for today's employees? And how should we say thank you?

There are an awful lot of details to consider. My 10 surefire ways to design a human workplace are based on what I've seen in my decades of work as a management consultant and my time spent as a researcher and writer, visiting and studying companies around the country. Believe me, I've seen it all. I've met dazed and confused management teams; wise-beyond-their-years entrepreneurs; sleepy corporate bureaucrats; nimble, innovative, inspiring executives; and everything in between. Through hundreds of interviews with CEOs, founders, managers, and employees, I've noticed trends, themes, common errors, and keys to success. So what follows is what I have distilled to be the macro, micro, glamorous, and nitty-gritty things that get results when you bring them to work.

Let's remember: just as no two humans are alike, no two companies are alike. While there are 10 surefire ways to approach the challenge of the human workplace, depending on the needs of your company and your stage of growth, you can pick and choose areas to focus on. If you are one of the lucky ones starting from scratch, you can build a human workplace from the ground up. If you have a specific problem with meetings or questions about technology or professional development, for example, you can pick up tips from the chapters that speak to you.

With that said, Chapter One—Be Real: Speak in a Human Voice—is a must for everyone. In this chapter, I tackle the importance of finding your company's real voice and appreciating the value of values—two of the most important steps in creating a human workplace.

Peppered throughout the book, I shine a spotlight on people, places, and things to help you on the road ahead. At the end of the day, only you know what your workplace needs. By the time you are finished with this book, I hope you will see that whether you want to start a business, grow your current one, recruit the best and the brightest to work for you, or just feel more connected all around, bringing your human to work is good for people, great for business, and just might change the world.

1

Be Real: Speak in a Human Voice

Ellen Bennett, a self-described "millennial with an old soul," struts across the conference stage, describing how five years ago she wanted to "make the world a better place." "All I had was my phone," she tells the audience. Fast forward to today's event: the New York City 2015 Tech Table Summit, a collection of leaders and tastemakers in hospitality, and this proud, f-bomb-dropping, totally pumped CEO has taken the stage. Her company, Hedley & Bennett, is the go-to purveyor of chic aprons, outfitting pro and DIY foodies around the world. How did one young woman turn something as ho-hum as a kitchen apron into a booming lifestyle brand, worn and loved by employees in over 5,000 restaurants and hotels worldwide?

As Bennett puts it, "Be real, and encourage other people to be real." Sounds easy enough. But what does it mean to "be real"? What does being real have to do with launching a successful business? As Bennett explains, when she started making aprons, all she had was her phone and herself. It was only "fitting" that her product would be infused with her special touch and her naturally sparkly personality—there wasn't anything getting in her way! Admittedly, not all companies are cut from such personable cloth. Yet regardless of a founder's temperament, the product, or the available resources, the same principle applies: authenticity is good for business.

While I invite readers to pick and choose from the 10 chapters in this book to find what works for them, this chapter is first for a reason. In order for a human company to flourish, it has to be genuine, aligned, and true to itself. A real company actually flaunts its humanity; it doesn't hide it. More and more, customers of all ages are flocking to authenticity[1] and so are employees.

In fact, in a 2013 study, professors from Harvard University, the London Business School, and the University of North Carolina discovered that when companies emphasize newcomers' "authentic best selves" over an organizational identity, this emphasis leads to greater employee retention and customer satisfaction within six months.[2]

In this chapter, I share three ways smart companies are bringing their human to their brands by being real.

Know Your Brand's Values

Even if you haven't taken the time to sit down with your employees to articulate and communicate your company's set of values, one thing is for sure: these values drive everything you and your company do, whether you're aware of their impact or not. The thing about values is that they are hard at work, calling the shots of your business, even when they are implicit. That's why it's so important to make our values seen and heard.

Learning How to Live by Values
at JetBlue University

It's Wednesday in Orlando, Florida. Outside the windows of this building, located a few miles from the airport, the sky is grey, but the auditorium is bright and lively. One by one, 176 people stand up and share their story:

My name is Mickey. I'm from Jamaica, and I used to be a bartender at Madison Square Garden.

My name is Gloria. I'm from Minnesota, and I've worked in child services and luxury retail.

My name is Jonah, and I'm an actor, but my dog made it onto Broadway before I did.

The crowd—mostly a thirtysomething, cosmopolitan mix of extroverts and charmers—cracks up. They are asked to hold their applause between introductions, but their enthusiasm makes it hard.

When I was invited to attend the new-hire orientation at JetBlue University, I had no idea what I was getting myself into. For anyone new to the crew, the experience is the same—total Blue-Juice indoctrination. "Drinking the Blue Juice" is how Jet-Blue folks refer to their training.

To be honest, I didn't really understand all this amped-up team spirit at first. Then I heard, again and again, from all over the map at JetBlue:

After a career in aviation, this has been my dream: to have a job at JetBlue.

I love my job here at JetBlue and hope it's my last.

My name is Amanda, and before JetBlue, I was a nobody.

As the leader-in-residence (the JetBlue executive who serves as an emcee during the training) announced at the first night's pep rally, "We're kind of a cult!"

After studying this feisty, highly disciplined company of 21,000 crew members, it became clear to me that their success had nothing to do with size or innovative technical brilliance like that of Google or Apple. They have only 5 percent of seats traveling in the air, yet their revenue over the 10 years ending in December 2016 grew almost 3x, far out-pacing the revenue growth of the industry.[3] And, size notwithstanding, JetBlue has become one of the most iconic brands in the world. How did they do it? It's actually super simple and completely within reach for all of us.

Like Ellen Bennett's aprons, so clearly distinguishable from ordinary aprons, JetBlue also has a strong, very human, and very approachable brand identity. As a Johnson & Johnson executive asked a JetBlue leader at a meeting on innovation, "You guys have managed to be an airline associated with love. How on earth do you do that?"

It starts with their values.

At this recent orientation, Brad Sheehan, vice president of JetBlue University, described the company values to his 176 new crew members like this:

Safety—We want our crew members to feel safe, so we take care of them physically and mentally.

Integrity—We do the right thing when no one is looking.

Caring—If we can be nice to each other, it is easier to be nice to our customers.

Passion—The fuel that drives us to come to work. While we can't control gas prices (one type of fuel), we can hire for and control the other kind of fuel.

Fun—How you bring your personality to JetBlue and make it to work. We want you to bring what we saw in you to work every day.

Leader after leader, speaking to the group, emphasized these values, describing them as the underpinnings of everything the company does. According to Executive Vice President and Chief People Officer Mike Elliott, these values are the "glue" that holds JetBlue together. These dynamic speakers didn't just *tell* the group the values; they *showed* how the values came alive in story after story, in videos, and sometimes in a customer's own voice.

One unforgettable tale was told via an audio recording of a mother's voice. She recounted how she stood with her developmentally delayed teenage son outside of the "family bathroom" near her gate, waiting for a key that never came. The situation was getting dire; the boy desperately needed to use the restroom. A JetBlue crew member found her and not only helped her get into a different bathroom appropriate for the young boy, but also helped the mother take hands-on care of the boy in a situation where most would have turned away to avoid such intimacy.

It goes without saying that no group of people will always be aligned, yet these JetBlue values are clearly heartfelt, and even more importantly, *always* top-of-mind. That's what it takes. Crew members are expected to have these values memorized, in the order they are listed and at the ready.

Truthfully, every time I fly JetBlue, I can see the values in real time. Recently I took a JetBlue flight from San Francisco to New York. After a long week of work, I was exhausted. Melvin, the lead crew member, welcomed us aboard and announced that he was going to be working with his best friend, James. Because I know the science showing that having friends at work makes us better at our jobs, I smiled. Everyone around me seemed more relaxed as well.

Later in the flight, I struck up a conversation with James. He had come from another airline and said that his experience at JetBlue was dramatically different. JetBlue is, he said, "a truly caring airline." He told me about the flowers he received from his boss after a death in the family and described how accommodating managers are about switching schedules to attend to personal business. He also told a story about a time he and Melvin got into a car accident one night while driving to their hotel after a day of flying. JetBlue sent a car with crew members to visit them at the hotel and to make sure they were okay. James said, "JetBlue takes such good care of me, and I am so grateful that I want to take care of my passengers and everyone around."

JetBlue just gets it. They know that relationships are key to any fundamental set of values, and moreover, they know how to honor a web of relationships. In order for employees to share these values with customers, they need to feel that they themselves are on the receiving end of the values. That is to say, for the in-flight crew to make folks on the plane feel safe, they themselves have to trust the pilot, ground operations, and leaders. Safety begets safety; integrity begets integrity; caring begets caring.

SPOTLIGHT

Ground Control Brings Culture to Airbnb

Airbnb's brand is all about creating a sense of belonging, and not just for their guests and hosts. They actually have a group of employees (10 people in San Francisco and someone in almost every office around the world) whose role it is to take the values off the walls and into the halls. Similar to the role of ground control in an airline, the group takes care of the office environments, events, internal communications, employee recognition, celebrations, and even the design of the office. According to Mark Levy, the former head of employee experience, these people aren't "forcing fun, they're reinforcing and supporting how we bring the culture alive." Levy says, "They do it through pop-up birthday celebrations, anniversaries, or baby showers as well as creative themed events based on holidays or events—whether it's Pride or the launch of their entry into Cuba."[4] This is the kind of effort it takes to truly scale culture.

Lyft Puts Values in the Driver's Seat

The ride-sharing market is worth billions and was originally dominated by Uber. Then along came Lyft, a San Francisco–based ride-sharing company identified by a glowing pink moustache on the front dash. How did they manage to break into the space?

They let their values drive them, that's how.

An article on Medium illustrating the differences between Lyft and Uber notes, "[A] key difference between the two companies' cultures is that Lyft passengers are encouraged to sit in the front seat and engage in conversation, while Uber operates more like a traditional taxi service, where passengers sit in the back seat and mind their own business."[5] That is to say, Lyft emphasizes human connections. Lyft's mission is "to reconnect people through transportation and bring communities together." It sounds lofty, but a mission has to be. Like any strong brand, Lyft knows that developing and embracing core values is the way to manifest that mission, however aspirational it may be. Their official core values apply to passengers, drivers, and employees alike:

Be Yourself. Great communities start with great individuals. Live authentically, and trust your voice.

Create Fearlessly. Challenge convention, take risks, and make an impact. If it's broken, fix it. If it doesn't exist, invent it.

Uplift Others. Invest in kindness, and always put community first. Deliver delight, and be a force of good.

Make It Happen. Now. Life is short. Live up front.

How does a ride-sharing business bring these values to life? First, they hired someone to focus on it. Ron Storn joined Lyft as the vice president of people (he recently left), and it was his job to ensure that the values were felt throughout the organization—from welcoming employees' dogs to the office, to ensuring that each team has a budget to do community service work each month. Employees are hired based on these values, then evaluated and compensated on them as well. Each new employee receives a coffee card to take colleagues from other teams out for "coffee and conversation." To oversee it all, a rotating Culture Board was established. Everyone involved should have input into how to improve and scale the culture.

Which is to say, Lyft gives its customers more than just a ride; it literally puts its values in the driver's seat.

Both JetBlue and Lyft lead with their values, building the very fundamentals of their company mission around them. This creates a clear direction for leaders to manage their teams, and it inspires employees to be engaged. Having such a distinctive purpose, laid out in a clear set of values, is just good business.

Speak in an Authentic Voice

Once a company knows who they are and what their values are, that identity must be shared with customers, employees, and the world. This is a company's voice, and like all voices, it must be heard. In order to breathe life into a brand, companies need to confidently broadcast what that brand stands for. Smart companies take pains to establish their voice systematically and meticulously, over the lifespan of the business.

Telling stories—personal stories, professional stories, and brand stories—is the perfect vehicle for expressing the truth of your company's brand. Stories are free, are always available, and are such a core part of our human DNA that they automatically make us feel good. Especially when they're true. Best of all, when a company brings true stories to light, the culture becomes more attentive to stories, and it's a virtuous cycle. Leaders and managers learn to keep their eyes and ears on what's most important: the real experiences of real people.

Union Square's Honest Hospitality

People have always considered honesty to be one of our most valued virtues in the study of philosophy and ethics. The old adage goes, honesty is the best policy. And when it comes to bringing your human to work, it's an absolute must.

Erin Moran, a seasoned, successful consultant, is the very first chief culture officer at Danny Meyer's Union Square Hospitality Group (USHG), an immediate signal that this company—a high-profile, trendsetting restaurant group—is getting serious about bringing their human to work. Which makes sense. Meyer's business strategy is based on what he calls "enlightened hospitality." When I asked him what prompted him to hire a CCO, he told me that ever since he realized that any good business is in a constant state of finding balance between an emphasis on finance and on culture, he wanted a culture officer to work alongside the chief financial officer. "I could have named it anything . . . chief storyteller," he said. And chief storyteller would have been an apt title for Moran.

Moran and I met at the USHG headquarters in Manhattan just as an afternoon wine tasting was winding down. Moran is warm, a great listener, and smiles easily. After sharing her story about how she ended up in this exciting position three short years ago, she revealed to me that after she accepted the job, she "had a panic attack," and actually said to Meyer, "I don't think this is a good decision anymore." Being a person of integrity (one of the USHG's "Family Values," and no doubt one of the qualities that Meyer found so appealing in Moran), she understood that it would be difficult, to say the least, to take care of the culture—and the people—in an industry where she had absolutely no experience. She also worried that she would have a hard time establishing credibility, never having waited a single table her entire life ("I was always working either in retail or in college as a teacher's assistant").

After Meyer convinced her that her outsider status was a benefit, Moran forged ahead, trying to establish rapport, gain insight, and develop programs that would keep the culture rich and meaningful and the employees happy. One of the most powerful experiences she's had in her three years as head of culture (or, as she confessed to me, perhaps in her entire career) was when she gave a talk on the topic of unity in front of the 125 employees of the Modern, a high-end restaurant owned by USHG. Sensing an opportunity, she decided to forgo the typical executive talking points on the value of unity and instead spoke in a real voice about herself and her challenges. According to

Moran, she was "completely open and vulnerable . . . own[ing] the fact that [she'd] never walked in their shoes."

She received a standing ovation and an overflowing inbox of praise. While Moran didn't say this, I can only imagine that she received a credibility spike from her employees as well.

SPOTLIGHT

The Schmutz Pact

Harry Gottlieb, the founder of Jellyvision, the maker of interactive benefits communication software ALEX and Jackbox Games, was having lunch with a good friend one day when she told him that he had a piece of food stuck in his beard and helped him wipe it off. When he thanked her for being the kind of friend who does such things, she said, "We have a Schmutz Pact, right? Like you tell me, and I'm going to tell you."

Schmutz is a Yiddish or German word for dirt or grime. We all know how valuable friends who will save us from our schmutz are. Not so long after that conversation, Gottlieb sent out an all-company email inviting folks to participate in an "old time Chicago-style ballot stuffing" to help a friend win votes for an internet contest. A brave programmer named Jeremy wrote him an email, ever so tactfully suggesting that Gottlieb was, inadvertently of course, asking the staff to cheat. Obviously Gottlieb was "horrified!"

And grateful.

At the next all-hands meeting, Gottlieb stood up and praised Jeremy, explaining that's "what a friend does: he doesn't shame you when there's something wrong. He assumes you don't even know there's a problem and points out the issue in a kind, collegial way." And this is when Gottlieb announced the importance of their companywide Schmutz Pact, a catchy phrase for what he used to call "being honest and kind at the same time."

An Empire of Personal Touch

Competition is fierce in every industry, and food and lifestyle brands are no exception. One way to stand out from the crowd is to be truly authentic, by leaving your fingerprints on everything you do. Showcasing this personal touch is not just a "nice to have," it's a powerful business strategy.

When it comes to combining personal touch with business, Food52 is one such company that gets it right. Food52, founded by Amanda Hesser and Merrill Stubbs in 2009, is a strong competitor in the online food and lifestyle space and an early devotee of sincerity and authenticity as part of their brand. What started as a hotline for everyday home cooks (all 52 weeks in a year, get it?) is now a booming brand with a line of cookbooks, a podcast, an online shop with more than 2,000 kitchen and home goods, a series of offline pop-ups, and an audience of 12 million across platforms. In a 2016 article, *New York Magazine* referred to the company as "an empire." Yet one of their official core values is *Personal Touch: We treat everyone in our community with warmth and care, and we make sure they know there are real people behind the scene*s, and they take this very seriously.

The first time we talked, Hesser explained to me that since their primary interest is food, which is "so personal and inherently social, and forever has brought people together," their aim was to "replicate that in a way that is productive and genuine online." This meant that they thought a lot about the personality of the community they wanted to create. Because online environments can feel like "they are literally in the cloud," Hesser and Stubbs set out to "break down that wall and let people know who [they] are and what [they're] up to, and allow people to make that kind of emotional connection with [them]."

When the two started out, they wrote handwritten thank-you notes to their early customers. Two thousand of them. Even today, they'll write notes to customers, purely to surprise and delight them. These days they also use Facebook Live and Instagram Live to share product reviews, giving people a peek behind the perfectly rumpled linen napkin. When I visited their bustling New York City office, I could see this reality principle clearly functioning among employees as well—all 70 of them styling photo shoots, chatting in one of the kitchens, or having a meeting in the lounge with their laptops. The natural light, big shared desks, simple lines, modern farm tables, and cubbies all add to the cozy factor, which is very high. As Hesser notes, "What we're trying to build is relationships with people."

It's working. Crain's just named Food52 one of the fastest growing businesses in New York City.

The honest hospitality of Erin Moran and USHG, and the deliberate, personal touch of Food52 are two smart approaches to making the human connections that employees and customers crave. And best of all, they don't cost a thing and will always be unique to your brand. Honesty and authenticity, by definition, will always be original.

Empower Employees to be
Brand Ambassadors

Once your company's values are defined, and your voice is articulated step-by-step through stories, notes, or whatever works, it's time to engage your employees in the brand's mission. As Danny Meyer said to me, "Your brand is never better than your employees. And your employees are never better than the degree to which they are engaged in the reason your company exists."

This "engagement" is what happens when an employee is in front of a customer. What happens when no one's looking? But should companies provide a script, guiding an employee's response based on values and voice? No way. That would be inauthentic and the opposite of a human interaction. Instead, employees need to be educated, mentored, supported, rewarded, and then *empowered*—it is up to them to bring their human to work with your mission in mind.

JetBlue Flies in Grey Skies

As we've seen, JetBlue is a human place to work. They honor relationships. Furthermore, their human values are infused in everything they do, and people like me can feel it. So how and why do *individuals* feel inspired to live the company's values and be brand ambassadors? It's one thing for the C-suite to contemplate these goals and strategies, but it's quite another for a crew member to manifest these strategies in real time. Someone can drink all the Blue Juice in the world and still not be able to incorporate it into their lives and into their interactions with customers. Therefore, JetBlue has all kinds of supportive scaffolding in place to help.

Kristen Heasley has been an in-flight crew member with JetBlue for over six years. When I chatted with her, we were

in the air, standing in the back of the plane after the compli-
mentary beverage service had been offered on our way back
from Orlando. I introduced myself and mentioned this book to
her. She and her partner, Angel Morse, both said what everyone I talked to said—that they love JetBlue, will never work for
another airline if they can help it, and they have a lot of fun.

The thing that really caught my attention while talking to
Kristen was a story about a gentleman on the plane—the very
plane we were on!—who was disturbed by a noise he heard
before takeoff. He was sitting in the exit row and became
agitated. Kristen asked him if he wanted to switch seats with
someone else and assured him that the noise was completely
normal. He insisted it was not normal and became increasingly
upset, even aggressive. Kristen reminded him that she was,
above all, responsible for the safety of the customers (Safety is
Value #1), even going so far as to ask him, "If I thought there
was a problem, do you think I'd be standing here so calmly?"
She informed him that if he couldn't calm down, he was going
to have to be escorted off the plane. I asked her how she handled that—if she was angry, annoyed, or resentful that she had
to deal with him.

"Not really," she answered. "I knew he was just scared."

JetBlue—not surprisingly—has a name for the kind of
boundary maneuvering Kristen had to navigate with her customer. They call it "JetGrey," which refers to the way JetBlue
empowers crew members to trust themselves and make decisions in real time, using their real voices and I-statements like
the one mentioned earlier. This says to the crew: *We trust your
judgment.* We trust *you.* We actually *want* you to bring your
human to work. This allows the other aspects of customer service to shine through, like being truly helpful and empathetic.
And fun!

Speaking of fun, I would be totally remiss if I didn't mention what a blast it looks like the crew is having, or the hilarious, even cheeky jokes they crack over the speaker. For example, at the end of one of Kristen's colleague's long list of dos and don'ts and safety features, she added, "And for those traveling with more than one child, please pick your favorite." I laughed along with all of the other passengers.

SPOTLIGHT

Living on Purpose

After suffering an anxiety attack while operating a plane, as well as having a career on Wall Street that left him "successful, but without joy," Karan Rai, CEO of the financial services firm Asgard Partners & Co., realized that something needed to change. He was not living in alignment with his purpose. He founded Asgard Partners & Co. to create a life "more in harmony" with who he wanted to be, personally and professionally. And it's working.

As a matter of fact, Rai believes that most people have it backwards and that we need to start making a "business case for purpose." He invests in companies with strong financials (that is a given as he has to provide returns to his investors), but he only invests in companies that have a "higher purpose." In other words, the success of their business will also be good for the world.

Now that's putting your money where your mouth is.

Empowering Employees to "UpLyft" Others

As one ride-sharing blogger writes, "Drivers are the new bar-tenders." This is so true! We spend a lot of time with our drivers these days. Since a core value at Lyft is Uplift Others, it is up to employees to actually do this important heavy "lyfting." One of the most incredible stories—ever—is about a driver who picked up a passenger on Valentine's Day and handed the passenger a card that read "Be My Valentine." The passenger started cry-ing. The driver pulled over, turned the meter off, and talked with her, and when she seemed ready, the driver took her to her destination.

A few weeks later a friend of the passenger wrote to Logan Green, Lyft's CEO, with quite a message: "Your driver saved my friend's life." Apparently, that passenger was contemplating suicide, and that human touch made her reconsider. If employ-ees are not empowered to manifest company values in their own way, they will never have the opportunity to make the true con-nections that really matter.

Another great UpLyft story was also told during an all-hands meeting. A woman recounted the story of the Lyft driver who drove her daughter to safety away from a violent roommate, and actually helped her unpack her belongings into a hotel room. A picture of the driver's smiling face appeared on the screen behind her as the choked-up mother described the impact this man's kindness had on her and her family. According to Ron Storn, the former vice president of people, this story highlights more than the driver's determination to "uplift others." Through sharing the story publicly, all of Lyft's employees get uplifted as well.

There is nothing in an employee handbook that could have instructed someone to have the heart and mind to reach out and help customers in these ways.

Except maybe, *bring your human to work. Please*?

🤝 HUMAN ACTION PLAN

Take Your Values Off the Walls and into the Halls!

1. **Define your values.** Your values guide you and represent who you are and what your company stands for. A great litmus test to determine them is when you find yourself at a fork in the road, making an important, strategic decision such as deciding whether or not to hire a key team member, your values should help you figure out what to do. My rule of thumb is to pick four to six values. This magical number forces leaders to identify the most important goals to focus on and is an easy number of values for employees to remember.

2. **Align these values with all parts of your business.** Your values should help determine everything from who you hire to how you develop and promote employees. They should dictate how you communicate to employees, customers, and business partners via all mediums (text, email, phone, and face-to-face).

3. **Shine a light on employees who live the values.** Living values is often defined as what employees do when no one is watching. For example, those times when a Lyft driver or a JetBlue crew member is going the extra mile to help a customer. To empower employees to live your company's

values, you need to celebrate, share, and communicate when you find employees who are doing just that. This teaches other employees what it looks like and reinforces the importance of sustaining a strong culture and keeping the values off the walls and in the halls.

2

Play the Long Game: True Sustainability Is a State of Mind

Pursuing a sustainability agenda is a natural extension of our mission, because it means making sure that the communities we serve are healthy and resilient.
—**MARNE LEVINE**, COO of Instagram[1]

Not long ago, the word *sustainable* conjured images of recycling tree huggers, people who were so focused on saving the planet and its critters that they lost sight of us bipeds. Today, the concept of sustainability has evolved to include all the inhabitants of the earth, and a human workplace is about creating an ecosystem of sustainability for all of us. There's a lot at stake here, folks—this surely impacts our businesses, but in many respects it affects even our future as a species.

That's right. If you want your company to last, you have to think about the future. While this might sound obvious, the future is more difficult to consider than we may care to admit. Remember the "marshmallow test"? Way back in 1960, scientists at Stanford University placed a marshmallow in front of little kids and explained to the kids that if they could wait fifteen minutes to eat it, they would be rewarded with two marshmallows. Ultimately, the kids who could delay gratification ended up being generally more successful in their lives, even scoring higher on the SAT.[2]

Sustainability is like the marshmallow test for business. I call it playing the long game, and playing the long game is not easy. In the original marshmallow study, only 30 percent of the kids held out for their second treat.

A truly human, thriving workplace has to do better than that. We want the treats on the table to grow over time.

Not only is investing in the future the right thing to do for the world and your company, but top talent is also looking for companies that are willing to embrace sustainability. As a matter of fact, they are demanding it. Nathaniel Koloc, cofounder and CEO of ReWork, a mission-driven talent firm that connects professionals to hiring managers, wrote in a 2013 *Harvard Business Review* article:

> *We've heard from associates at all the big management consultancies, analysts at the largest investment banks, developers at the most prominent technology companies, and senior managers from Fortune 50 corporations, and they all tell us the same things. They are not picking their next job based on the size of the paycheck. They are instead looking for a worthwhile mission and promising team to join.[3]*

This is especially true of millennials, who in my opinion are making the workplace more human for all of us by insisting on getting more from work than just a paycheck.

Satya Nadella is the CEO of Microsoft, credited with more than doubling the company's stock growth by focusing on culture.[4] He takes the long game seriously. Because of his success, Nadella fields a lot of questions about how things are going now, and he says, "My response is very Eastern: we're making great progress, but we should never be done. This is a way of being."[5]

What does it mean to transform a company through a way of being? It means being aware of one's state of mind and intention. Playing the long game requires changing the way we think about everything. Which might explain why a 2016 survey by Bain & Company established that just 2 percent of companies achieve their own sustainability goals.[6]

Make Work Practices Intentional

To stay ahead of the curve—to play the long game—we must craft vital, intentional work practices that account for the complexity of people's real lives. This crafting must consider all the people our business impacts, which means all stakeholders, including our employees, our customers, and our partners. The long game is broad and inclusive, spanning our macro and micro spheres of influence.

Let's start with the ground-level, employee experience, and the way we ask people to spend their days. The days of one-size-fits-all 40-hour work weeks, with two weeks of vacation and maybe a little flex time when absolutely necessary, are over. Top talent is demanding a more human schedule. So what does that look like?

Everyday Flexibility

Deloitte's recent millennial study summed up what this new generation wants in one sentence: "Freelance flexibility with full-time stability."[7] Another study undertaken by the IBM Smarter Workforce Institute and Globoforce's WorkHuman Research Institute involving more than 23,000 employees in 45 countries determined that when employees agree their work schedule is flexible enough to meet family and other personal responsibilities, 79 percent report a more positive employee experience.[8] Perhaps these millennial types are on to something.

That's a pretty powerful number. How do we craft the kind of intentional work practices that create positive employee experiences? Technology has made certain aspects of progress look so easy. Much of our work can be done virtually, but what happens to our company culture when we're texting from home or from the local Starbucks? One of the most common (and passionate) conversations I have with employees and leaders is about balancing the perks of technology with a strong and related corporate culture. Don't we have to be in the office to create that glue of connection?

Yes, we do, to some extent. Which is why we can't just throw out a willy-nilly, "work from home whenever you like" model and see what happens. We have to be strategic in our flexibility.

By way of example, I love the way Food52, an online life-style platform devoted to creating community around food, does it. They want their employees to be in the office to connect with each other, but they also understand the importance of taking care of other business. To achieve this important balance, they choose to be concrete and intentional about how and when employees work from home. They call it Workday Wednesday and they lay it out in the employee handbook:

Food52 team members have the option to work from home on Wednesdays when needed. This way, people who really must work from home can do so, and there will be fewer days that people miss each other. And, of course, we know there are occasional emergencies, like having to take delivery of your great aunt Bessie's grand piano, and we're happy to be flexible when these occasions arise.

Similarly, Raytheon, an innovator in defense and cybersecurity solutions, implemented a popular program called the 9/80, which allows employees to work nine-hour days and get every other Friday off. This way, employees can "take care of personal business, see family, travel, take a dance class, and have a life outside of work."

At HubSpot, an inbound marketing company with more than 2,000 employees, flexibility is the rule, not the exception. "We recognize that every individual is unique in how they'd like to spend time with their family, friends, or on other personal pursuits," explains cofounder and CTO Dharmesh Shah. "We've found that a self-driven and positive employee experience is deeply connected to customer success."[9] According to the vice president of human resources, Elissa Barrett, flexibility is an intentional part of HubSpot's culture: "It's something that is talked about all the time to ensure that the decisions we are making are aligned with our company values." Barrett shared with me that in her first week of work at HubSpot, Chief People Officer Katie Burke left a copy of the book *Remote* on her desk. Barrett thought to herself, "Okay. Game on. Let's do this." In one of their initial meetings, Burke asked Barrett, "What kind of schedule works for you?" When people throughout the company constantly talk about flexibility and what works versus what doesn't, they stay connected and build relationships with each other and the company.

These examples represent thoughtful, intentional approaches to those everyday things that come up in our lives. Flexibility is even more important when things get hard for people, for instance at the beginning and at the end of life.

SPOTLIGHT

Parting Ways Gracefully

"So here you are. You've just joined Jellyvision (or you've been working here for a while), and we want to talk about the END of your employment here? What's up with that?"

That is the beginning of the Graceful Leave Policy at Jellyvision, the maker of interactive benefits communications software ALEX and Jackbox Games. The idea is that each person Jellyvision hires is so valuable, and finding a replacement is so tricky, that out of respect, Jellyvision asks employees to notify the company when they start to look for a new job, apply to school, etc. In exchange for this respect, employees will get the support of Jellyvision in their job search, contacts and introductions, résumé assistance, and even prorated compensation.

Talk about transparent!

After an employee shares such wishes with Jellyvision, he or she will continue to be staffed on projects that "make sense" given the timing of departure (some former "Jellypeople," as they are called, have stayed on for more than six months), and employees are expected to work hard until the end. Parting ways is never easy, but at Jelly-vision it's done with the human touch.

Taking Care of Families

Parental leave is one of the most obvious intentional approaches. Shelley Zalis, founder of the Girls' Lounge and the Female Quotient, explained that "the rules in the workplace were written over 100 years ago by men for men. Women were not in the workforce." Zalis insists that to create a human workplace, we must "think about mandatory parental leave so it includes everyone."

Airbnb, whose tagline is "Belong Everywhere," has adopted a human, family-friendly mindset. Airbnb provides a minimum of 10 paid weeks of what they call "child bonding leave," inclusive of both new birth mothers and fathers, and parents of adopted children. They go even further, knowing how tricky it is to return after a long time away nesting. To ease the pain, Airbnb implemented a transition plan where employees can work 80 percent of the time for 100 percent pay for a few weeks before returning full-time. (How awesome would it be if schools did that for our kids after a summer break?)

Airbnb understands that, even with 10 weeks off, coming back to work with a baby at home can be really daunting. The thought of cooking dinner when you get home is sometimes just too much. To alleviate this stress, in those locations where food is offered, Airbnb invites new parents to take dinner home with them as part of their transition back to work. Finally, for mothers who are still nursing when they come back to work but have to travel, Airbnb will express-ship breast milk to wherever the mothers have to be. Nothing cookie-cutter about that! Airbnb puts its intentional workplace practices in place to benefit all of its parental employees.

Bring Your Baby to Work

While bringing your baby to work isn't a new concept, it surely isn't something particularly commonplace. Maybe it should be! Studies have shown that bringing a newborn to work leads to reduced stress for workers, higher retention, and improved productivity, especially when compared to the distracted state of new parents who are being separated from their newborns.[10]

Rose Marcario, CEO of Patagonia, is proud of the fact that "for 33 years, Patagonia has provided on-site child care—a mandate from our founders, who believed it was a moral imperative." Marcario adds, "Even in times of economic struggle, the program was never cut because [our founders] believed in providing a supportive work environment for working families." Does it cost money? Yes, it does. However, she says, "the good news for skeptical business leaders is something I've learned firsthand: supporting our working families isn't just the ethical thing to do (which, frankly, should be reason enough for responsible leaders); it will also balance out financially."[11]

In fact, Marcario estimates Patagonia recoups "91 percent of [their] calculable costs annually." This estimate does not account for the unseen benefits of such intentional, family-friendly programs. JPMorgan Chase bank, for example, estimates that its total return on investment (ROI) on its child care program is 115 percent. Plus, KPMG, a global consulting firm, "found that its clients earned a return on investment (ROI) of 125 percent."[12]

According to the World Bank Group's business case for employer-supported child care, "research shows that providing childcare benefits can boost the quality of a company's labor force by supporting the needs of a diverse workforce, improving recruitment, and helping to retain talent throughout the employee life cycle."[13]

Companies and workers alike benefit when the joys and struggles of new parenthood are supported through intentional work practices. Might the same be true when we are navigating through difficult life experiences as well?

SPOTLIGHT

How the Muse Brings Their Babies to Work

The Muse is a popular career-support destination. When cofounders Kathryn Minshew and Alexandra Cavoulacos read an article about a baby-at-work program, they knew that it needed to be a part of the Muse culture.

Here's how it works: employees can bring a baby to work for the first six months or until the baby starts crawling. Employees volunteer to be part of a "baby squad," people who watch the baby in situations that aren't ideal for a new baby. Squad members are required to attend an orientation meeting or be interviewed in advance. As Cavoulacos told me about her own experience bringing her baby to work, "Transitioning back to work after parental leave isn't easy—you're used to seeing your baby 24/7 and all of a sudden you're lucky to get more than an hour when she's awake. It's been really incredible to have the flexibility to bring my daughter into the office. I get to see her more, and it's made a real difference in child care costs for those few months."

Minshew put it well: "This policy—and others like it for parents and non-parents alike—allow people to feel supported rather than being stressed about going back to work as well."

And support is just what the doctor ordered for that long-game state of mind.

Standing by Employees During Difficult Times

Sheryl Sandberg, Facebook's COO, suffered an unfathomable loss when her husband died unexpectedly in 2015 during a vacation in Mexico. She experienced firsthand the pain of grief, and she also realized the importance of a company's support during these times. In coauthoring (with Adam Grant) her book *Option B: Facing Adversity, Building Resilience, and Finding Joy*, Sandberg noted that a three-day paid leave for bereavement is still common practice[14] and that in the United States, 40 percent of workers do not get any paid time off at all.[15]

Given her own experience mourning the loss of her husband, Sandberg has written about how to be sensitive to grieving friends.[16] Moreover, Sandberg has changed Facebook's policy from 10 to 20 days of bereavement leave, and with this intentional action, she has inspired many other corporations to do the same. In a Facebook post, she declared, "No one should ever have to choose between being a good family member and a good employee."[17]

Mastercard is one of the companies that listened. They recently increased their leave to 20 days. Sandberg wrote in her June 13, 2017, Facebook post, "Under CEO Ajay Banga and

Chief HR Officer Michael Fraccaro's leadership, Mastercard is sending a strong message to its employees: we'll stand by you during the most difficult moments of your life."

Sandberg continues, "You can't be successful unless you're committed to your employees—and if you are committed to them, they will be committed to you." Facebook and Mastercard stand out like other companies in this section as companies that are playing the long game by considering the broad life needs of their employees.

Which begets the question: Who *are* these employees?

SPOTLIGHT

Building Bridges at Accenture

In the summer of 2016, Darnell Thompson, an IT manager at Accenture, heard about two more shootings of unarmed black men. As the father of a young African American son, he was especially worried about his son's future. He described his feelings in a Facebook post: "The violence will continue until there is a culture change of perception of black people. We are not your enemies. We eat, drink, and breathe like you do, so why do you treat us so unjustly?"[18]

A number of Thompson's Facebook followers were colleagues from Accenture, including Ellen Shook, chief leadership and human resources officer. Thompson was Shook's "IT expert" and her "go-to" person for all things technical. When Shook saw Thompson's post, she was concerned. And she realized that if Thompson was feeling like this, so were many others at Accenture. Together with Julie Sweet, Accenture's CEO of North American operations, Shook hosted a live webcast with over 1,000 employees to discuss the issues we are facing as a country around diversity. This webcast turned into an Accenture program called Building Bridges, which is an open dialogue on diversity. Accenture strives to be a "truly human" company, and tackling these difficult conversations at work and paying attention to how all of their people are feeling is a critical part of being human.

Diversify and Include

Over the years, I have talked with a lot of incredible leaders about what it means to be in business for the long haul, and what it means to do it right. The folks in charge of the most inspiring companies are not running around with clipboards trying to check a million things off a million lists. Yes, they are productive, but more importantly, they are strategic and disciplined.

When it comes to cultivating diversity and inclusion, being strategic couldn't be more important. The old-school, simple bean counting based on race, ethnicity, or gender just won't do it anymore. The data is clear: studies reveal that truly heterogeneous teams (think age, race, gender, sexual orientation, work experience, technical expertise, and level of education) are more accurate and accountable than homogeneous ones.[19]

Adam Pisoni, a super-radical serial entrepreneur and founder of the education-tech startup Abl, became so convinced of the importance of having a diverse group at the foundation of his company that he risked breaking the law to get there. To achieve his company's uncommon diversity—of his 12 new hires, a majority were either women or people of color—his first round of recruiting was an explicit search for diversity.[20] Once someone became a candidate for Abl, his or her "status" fell away. Still, this bold ambition highlights the importance of diversity to Pisoni. Perhaps the risk was, and still is, worth it. Pisoni seems to thinks so. In response to the question if this is legal, Pisoni counters, "I'm not really sure. . . . If you ask a lawyer, he or she will probably say, 'Be careful.'"

Let's assume Pisoni is being careful. I can't say I blame him for taking his chances. After all, "companies with gender-diverse management teams have a 48 percent higher operating margin,"[21] and according to PwC, "85 percent of CEOs whose organizations have a diversity and inclusiveness strategy say it's enhanced performance."[22]

Seeking diversity, as Pisoni has, is one thing when a company is starting from scratch and is just getting off the ground. What about established companies with a large workforce? How can complex businesses incorporate diversity throughout their organizations?

EY Leans into the Bumpy

EY is a global professional services firm with 250,000 employees (over two-thirds of whom are millennials) in over 150 countries. It was named number one on DiversityInc's 2017 Top 50 Companies for Diversity list, "positioning it as the leading professional services firm for diversity and inclusiveness

(D&I)." As exciting as this was, it was nothing new for EY. For the previous nine years, EY had been in the top 10. Moreover, in terms of impact, companies included in DiversityInc's Top 50 have exceeded stock exchange performance by an average of 25 percent.[23]

When I caught up with Karyn Twaronite, global diversity and inclusiveness officer at EY, I asked her how they stay so ahead of the curve. First, she said, "tone starts at the top," something I have seen and heard again and again in my work with companies. To make that tone really mean something, Twaronite has been reporting to the CEO since 2011, suggesting that her efforts matter. In other words, at EY, diversity and inclusion is a front-and-center endeavor and not some under-the-radar, feel-good exercise. Twaronite told me, "We include D&I in every single function . . . so it's not like this little function of talent off to the side . . . 14 layers or levels under, that gets addressed as an afterthought. . . . Our management team has put D&I front and center . . . whether it's markets or finance or operations or risk or legal or talent."

The entire system is set up for success. Now what? Twaronite explains that they start—as we all should—with a road map, defining what D&I means at EY. Let's face it, if we don't know precisely what we're shooting for, we're pretty likely to miss it. With a topic as critical as diversity, we are taking one step toward the goal of more sensitive inclusion already by simply having thoughtful, data-rich, human conversations about what it actually means.

Twaronite knows this better than most. She mentioned, "There's a whole host of different complexities. But by calling it out, it has brought more people around the table to realize that diversity and inclusion programs and the investment is about them as well. It is about all of us."

More specifically, she expressed to me, "We include all the things that people typically think about, like gender, ethnicity, sexual orientation. But we also are very explicit to say different religions, different technical areas of acumen. Different work experiences. Different cultural upbringings. Different abilities, invisible or visible. Different working and communication styles." Again, the great news is that real diversity isn't just good for people. It's good for business. A study at the University of Michigan learned that a group of diverse problem solvers can outperform groups of high-ability problem solvers.[24] A subsequent *Forbes Insights* study[25] realized that workforce diversity and inclusion "is a key driver" of innovation and growth, and a 2013 study on gender diversity and innovation in R&D departments discovered "results [which] indicate that gender diversity is positively related to radical innovation."[26] These studies are consistent with yet additional research from McKinsey, whose 2015 work revealed that companies in the top quartile for "ethnic" diversity are 35 percent more likely to outperform their counterparts in the bottom quartile, and gender-diverse companies are 15 percent more likely.[27]

EY has witnessed this firsthand. For instance, they found that "if you have 30 percent women on a management team, across 90 countries, 22,000 companies, then you had six percentage points more in that margin, 15 percentage points more in revenues." Numbers like this make Twaronite's work incredibly gratifying. Still, creating and measuring intangible results isn't easy. Twaronite expressed, "We understand that [aligning with sameness] feels easier, faster, but we want and expect our people to lean into bumpy and to try to explore differences on their teams."

"Leaning into bumpy" is what it takes to effect change as we aim to bring our human to work. Challenging assumptions, creating new paradigms—this is important, impactful, bottom-line work. And it's *personal*. Consequently, we are bound to have personal, emotional—bumpy—reactions all along the way. Instead of letting the bumps throw us off, we must lean in and learn.

But how can we know if all our efforts, emotional and otherwise, are paying off? Twaronite noted that this is a "long-term, sustained investment, including through years like [the] financial crisis . . . [and] a whole host of other things." While economic benefits will surely come, as they have for EY, they might take some time to be revealed. Hopefully, in time, you will have so much impact under your belt that you can look back and identify your progress, as EY does. These days, success at EY is measured in many ways, but one radically simple metric shines through. They ask every single employee one question: Do you feel free to be yourself at work every day?

It sounds ridiculously simple. Even so, as with the most elegant solutions, it's incredibly powerful. Twaronite articulated:

> *We found that [this one question] is still directly, highly relevant, and we still can use it to measure how we are doing with respect to how our employees are feeling. And not only because it's about how an employee feels, but also it relates to how productive they are, how engaged they are. We have all the correlations as it relates to retention and turnover that you might expect. We've also seen a high level of correlation as to how well that business unit does, as well as how that business unit is rated by third parties, meaning how did the enterprise look from a branch perspective.*

When people feel like they can "be themselves at work," we all benefit.

Enlighten Your Supply Chain

On April 24, 2013, a five-story commercial building in Bangladesh called the Rana Plaza collapsed. More than 1,100 garment workers were killed and over 2,000 were injured. The prior year, factory fires in Pakistan and Bangladesh killed 350 workers and left many disabled.[28] These tragedies along with a list of similar tragedies led consumers to demand transparency from the garment industry.

These days, it's not just the garment industry that is under careful scrutiny for its humanity. Now, instead of caving to consumer pressure, companies are wearing their transparency on their sleeve, touting their corporate responsibility as part of their offerings. This makes for good business. In everything from toys to food, glasses, shoes, and more, companies are seeking ways to shine a light on their supply chains as part of what they're selling and who they are.

What was once just a means to an end (i.e., the factory, farm, or harvester) has become an index of how authentic or "real" a company is. Author Mike Doherty wrote way back in 2012 in an article for *Fast Company*: "There are many contributing factors, but the desire for 'real' seems to be driven by things that are bigger and more lasting than the usual 'trend and counter-trend' shifts that we often see."[29] Likewise, writer Eve Turow Paul observed in *Forbes* in 2016 that "slowly, these changes are pushing the supply chain to think more critically about their measures of 'success.'"[30]

Enlightened production here we come. It must be part of any forward-thinking company's planning. Let's examine some examples of this human thinking at work.

Happy Cows Make Better Ice Cream

Lori Joyce grew up an only child on a farm on Vancouver Island with her Croatian immigrant parents. Everything her family ate came from the farm, so she knew the origins and the stories of everything on her family's table. Intimately. Her milk was from her cow. Her eggs were from her chicken. Like the rest of us, Joyce didn't appreciate her childhood and the organic character of the food she was raised on until she became an adult.

As Joyce matured and began to food shop for her own children, she grew to appreciate how unusual and wonderful her food upbringing was. In the stores, she experienced persistent disappointment. She began to meticulously read food labels, but no matter how wholesome the ingredients appeared, she could never trace the food to its source the way she could during her childhood.

It turns out that Joyce has a major sweet tooth, and she particularly loves ice cream. Her ice cream label reading gave her a pretty shocking education. She soon discovered that most of what she was buying and eating from the frozen section didn't have enough butterfat to be called ice cream! They were more like "frozen desserts." Yuck!

This discovery got her thinking: "Why was there no premium ice cream brand made with farm-fresh, traceable cream and single-sourced ingredients?"[31] Enter Betterwith, "100 percent Honest Ice Cream."

Joyce knew her idea was a great one, and she found investors relatively easily. Finding traceable milk was much harder. At one point, after a few delays getting her product to market, her company board pushed her to just "get the product out" and *then* find the milk. She said no way. Traceability was the whole point! (See Chapter One's commitment to values.) Joyce had to contact Whole Foods and tell them her product would be late because she had not yet secured her milk source. Not an easy call for an entrepreneur to make.

But it turns out the world can be a pretty good place. Some partners actually play the long game. Whole Foods was so impressed by Joyce's commitment to transparency that they committed to carry her Betterwith ice cream whenever it was ready.

Two years later, Joyce found a farm where she could get the milk she was looking for—Lavender Farms in Abbotsford, British Columbia, a place where cows lollygag about and get milked when they feel the urge to purge. The farm uses a state-of-the-art milking system which invites cows to chow down on a healthy feed while they are being milked. What a life!

Joyce writes, "I was driving up to the farm and up the driveway, and it was so picturesque, from the green pastures and white fence to the beautiful family doing things very traditional and clean, with the highest respect for their animals."

It's that "highest respect" that Joyce was after, the feeling she wants stirred into each bite of her ice cream. "You can tell, when you walk onto a property, if those animals are happy. . . . If they approach you, if they look at you, or if they're intimidated, if they're scared. . . . Those cows were approachable and curious, and when animals are curious, they're comfortable and happy."[32]

Most importantly, as Joyce says, happy cows make better ice cream.

These days, sales are up, and her goal is to scale the business nationally in the years ahead. She is well on her way. Safeway just gave Betterwith dedicated freezer space, and demand is so high for her ice cream that she is already on the lookout for another farm.[33] Betterwith is all about the supply chain, and honoring relationships plays a big part in this better ice cream *moo*vement.

Thinking About Wine Inside the Box

Marian Leitner-Waldman and her husband Dave Waldman are both entrepreneurs but with different backgrounds—hers is in literature, his is in wine. They love bringing people together over food and drink to connect face-to-face in real time, old-school style. One of their favorite activities is hosting an "open dinner table" where anyone on a given night can stop by for a perfect combination of storytelling and culinary stimulation. It makes perfect sense that during a conversation about these dinner parties that the seed for Archer Roose, their up-and-coming boxed-wine disrupter, was planted.

Leitner-Waldman shared her story with me. "Dave was ribbing me about how much money I spent on wine that night. He reminded me that I was paying more for the shipping and packaging than the wine inside the bottle." This really struck her—as a consumer and an entrepreneur. Here was a problem that needed solving. How can wine be packaged in a way that shifts resources from bottles to grapes and helps the environment at the same time?

As Leitner-Waldman continued to "mull" (mulled wine . . . get it?) over this question, she looked around her very own table, and she saw her friends wearing Warby Parker glasses and Everlane clothes—two businesses with enlightened supply chains as a core part of their offerings. She thought to herself, "We're living in this age of revolution in the world of consumer goods. Why couldn't we do it in wine?"

She and Waldman had an epiphany. They realized it didn't need to be a bottle that they spent their packaging money on. The boxed-wine playing field was wide open, and they saw an empty spot on the shelf with their names on it. Boxed wine is also better for the environment.[34]

But of course! Let's call this an Enlightened Supply Chain light-bulb moment. The couple wrote on their website, "For us, it's not enough to simply make good wine. We want our wine to do good, too."

How does wine "do good," you might ask?

Well, for starters, its producers do no harm. In the name of 100 percent transparency, anyone can go to the Archer Roose website and learn how the wine ends up in the glass. Leitner-Waldman and Waldman only partner with people who espouse the highest standards. In their field this includes paying close attention to care for workers, treatment of soil, and types of additives in the wine. In addition, they "do well by doing good," donating a percentage of their profits to help rural entrepreneurs in the countries they source from through a partnership with Root Capital, an award-winning nonprofit investment group.

A brand like Archer Roose demonstrates that the time is right for a change of mindset and to take the long game seriously. Here, some out-of-the-box supply chain thinking ironically led to some in-the-box liquid success. Archer Roose reports that its 2017 revenue grew by over 250 percent from 2016. Let's all drink to that!

Making work practices intentional, becoming a champion for true diversity, enlightening your supply chains—these might seem like just another list of things to do, but once you change your state of mind, you will see that the long game is the only game in town. Being human is not just for the employees under a company's roof. A long-game state of mind means honoring all the relationships connected to our business—not only the people we work beside at the office every day, but also the people, animals, land, and natural resources affected by what we do.

🤝 HUMAN ACTION PLAN

Being sustainable is the key to making your workplace human. Playing the long game is just that—LONG. It can feel overwhelming and be hard to know where to start. But don't worry—you don't have to do it all at once.

1. **Begin with your values**. If you aren't sure where to start, start with your values (see Chapter One). If you value a diverse workforce, start analyzing your policies and practices to get an idea of just how diverse your company is. If you value transparency, have a sit-down with your business partners to discuss their values and your own. This will help ensure that their values and practices are consistent with yours.

2. **Ask your employees**. When in doubt, ask your employees what is important to them. Millennials value different things than Gen Xers, and Gen Xers want different things than Baby Boomers. Work practices may differ based on company size, geography, and whether or not your employees work on-site or remotely. Don't waste your time or money providing a program that employees don't want or value.

3. **Make a human-business case**. As you read in this chapter, playing the long game is good for people and good for businesses of all sizes. You

don't have to be Facebook or Google to implement intentional work practices or hire diverse candidates. Some programs do have an associated cost, but the cost of losing a great employee because he or she can't work from home one day a week or take time off to care for a sick parent is much higher. Playing the long game always wins.

3

The Sweet Spot: Finding That Special Something Between Tech and Connect

These days, technology, at the very least, plays a supporting role in pretty much everything we do and especially in how we communicate. Our communication options for making ourselves heard are dizzying, but they are not all created equal. We need to think of how we communicate as being along a continuum. Today, we have quick-exchange platforms such as Snapchat, WhatsApp, IM, and text messaging on one end, email kind of in the middle (amazing, huh?), snail mail further down the line, and at the very end, the old-school reliability of picking up the phone, walking across the hall, making a lunch date, or even hopping on a plane.

To figure out which mode of communication is best, it's important to think about what you are trying to convey. Are you five minutes late to drinks with a colleague? Go ahead and send a text. If you are an hour late to a meeting with your boss, you better pick up your phone and make a call. If you want to forge a new working relationship, influence someone, or close a deal, make that investment in some serious face-to-face time.

So as a rule of thumb, match the medium to the message. The higher the stakes, the more we should invest.

In any given situation, ask yourself: "What is the best medium of communication to honor this relationship?" We can't always jump on a plane to meet up with our customers, clients, staff, or partners the way we might like to. Is it reasonable then to leverage what's best about technology to help us honor our relationships? Sure it is. In other words, we must understand the trade-offs and how to find the sweet spot between tech and connect.

If you've read this far, you understand that great businesses run on the power of connection. If we let technology serve as a stand-in for real, *human* relationships, we miss the point. Big time. Not only is digital friending, following, liking, and sharing a far cry from real-time relating, we all know from our own daily experiences that technology can complicate and even impede our relationships with those we love. Digital discipline is important for all of us to practice, personally and professionally.

We must know when to put technology in its place—this could be in a basket at the center of the conference table or in your own handbag. And we must know how to design ways for it to work its magic without compromising our relationships. Smart businesses are getting serious about finding that sweet spot, and you should do the same.

High-Tech for Human Touch

Finding the sweet spot is a tricky balance. Ensuring that the *right* technology is in position is a great place to start. Don't use just any old widget. Mike Elliott, JetBlue's chief people officer, explained to me that the best method is to get rid of anything that does "not need that much human interaction, and then [use] that void . . . to do more of the human interaction."

JetBlue Trades Tasks for Small Talk

From the very beginning of a JetBlue crew member's career, the training is oriented toward human connection. JetBlue's mission is to "inspire humanity." The company's five very human values and well-branded lingo (words like "bluemanity") really help keep this human goal top-of-mind. JetBlue is willing to look at every single thing they do through a human lens.

Therefore, it makes sense that as early as new-hire orientation, they are experimenting with ways to make the JetBlue experience as human as possible. Elliott explained to me that, as might be expected in this industry, "there's a lot of paperwork just to get an employee on board" (excuse the pun). While JetBlue makes every effort to make employee onboarding a reasonably pleasant experience, there's always a dose of "you didn't get this, you didn't dot this *i*, you didn't cross this *t*, this photo is not good," which doesn't exactly inspire the feeling of connection.

So the orientation team makes every effort to automate all of the mundane tasks of orientation, such as filling out forms, either before attendees arrive or as the days unfold. When I spoke to Elliott, JetBlue was on the fourth or fifth run-through of its revamped-with-humanity-in-mind, biweekly orientation.

(Yep! JetBlue holds new-hire orientation *every two weeks*.) Elliott asked the person running the orientation, "How did the automation [go]—did it handle the stress test?" This is JetBlue code for "how did the new process work in real time?" The person running the orientation responded by telling him, "It worked great . . . the employees were interacting more." Elliott then explained to me that, with the new automated process, the team "felt better about [the orientation] because they were actually making small talk and building relationships with these new hires."

JetBlue gets it. You only get one chance to make that first impression with your new employees. You'd be well served to make it human.

SPOTLIGHT

Calling All Troops at Airbnb

Airbnb is all about importance of belonging, so I was not surprised to learn that every year or two the company invests in bringing its 3,000 employees together for one big three-day Airbnb lovefest. In light of the company's fast growth, the leaders demonstrated a commitment to maintaining and enhancing culture when they asked themselves: "If we are going to bring all of these people together from around the world, how are we going to make sure that they get to know and spend time with people that they typically wouldn't be with?"

They turned to data. Airbnb's team created an algorithm to bring together groups of six people, who were not likely to know one another, into what they called a troop. Then they curated opportunities for troop members to connect throughout the conference. Troops grabbed their badges together, ate together, and sat together at the keynote. At the end of the event, they sat together at the 3,000-person family dinner. That's a lot of togetherness that would never have happened if Airbnb had not used big data to form small groups—quite the sweet spot strategy.

Tag—Who's It?

Walking up to the ticket agent at the airport was once a routine (and even exciting) part of the travel experience. Back in the day, this was a time to exchange pleasantries and amp up the excitement of a big trip. More recently, this interaction has gone the same way as too many customer service experiences and now feels stiff, rushed, and sometimes even hostile. As a result, when JetBlue introduced self-serve kiosks, some customers loved how these slick ATM-like machines helped them save time and avoid an unnecessary trip to the counter. Others, though, flustered and frustrated by having to print their own bag tags and check themselves in, felt like they were witness to the utter demise of civilization.

Joanna Geraghty, JetBlue's executive vice president of customer experience, has set out to please both types of customers—those comfortable with tech and those who prefer the old-school ways of engagement. Her goal is to automate those features that don't *require* a personal touch by using self-serve kiosks for check-in and bag tagging, so crew members have more time to identify the people who really do need (or simply want!) the help, thereby deepening those connections. This means that crew members have more time to help passengers by doing things like grabbing coffee for an overtired mother "traveling alone with three kids . . . [who are] all three, four, and five years old, and running in different directions" (a true story I heard during my research), and ensuring that customers in need of wheelchairs get the extra TLC they require to make it safely to their gates. Once crew members were freed up from checking people in, and from being tangled in bag tags, they had more time to take care of the customers' needs. And, importantly, JetBlue celebrates those efforts.

Let's be honest. It would be ideal if we could do it all—tag everyone's bag with a smile and take care of each and every customer with equal attention. But for companies looking for ways to improve performance *and* the bottom line while looking for balance in their embrace of technology and customer engagement, JetBlue is a powerful example of using technology wisely and well.

SPOTLIGHT

Recruiting Robots That Find the Sweet Spot at Jellyvision

Jellyvision, the Chicago-based benefits communications software maker and Jackbox Games creator, strives not only to be real and authentic in business (remember the Schmutz Pact?), but also to find the sweet spot. It starts during the recruiting process, when candidates get their first glimpse into Jellyvision's quirky and casual culture. Mary Beth Wynn, Jellyvison's senior vice president of people, introduced me to their recruiting robot, a trained, response-generating counterpart in the recruiting process. The robot serves, essentially, as the company's brand ambassador, which, as we learned in Chapter One, is an important way to Be Real.

In response to talent inquiries, the bot first sends a timely auto response to introduce himself and connect. Thereafter, candidates are kept abreast of their status in the process, with humor interlaced throughout: "Thank you for sending in your résumé to Jellyvision. I don't have any pull around here, but I'm rooting for you!" Explains Wynn, "The tone of our emails is fun and casual (like our culture)."

Setting the Table and the Tone

A recent paper by Bain & Company, the global consulting firm, paints quite the picture of how businesses will function in 2027:

> *Firms will combine big data, which will be pervasive, with human intelligence from frontline interactions with customers, and the resulting information will all be instantly visible throughout the company. Transactional activity will be almost entirely automated; algorithms and machine learning will simultaneously reduce the need for routine interactions while opening up new avenues for customer engagement.*[1]

This is the sweet spot we're talking about and what JetBlue is already working toward. Which makes sense, as JetBlue is a big, powerful Fortune 500 "firm." But what does the sweet spot look like in other industries?

Union Square Hospitality Group Honors Human Beings

One of my all-time favorite sweet spot stories is of a Shake Shack employee catching wind of a loyal pair of customers on a tour of every Union Square Hospitality Group (USHG) establishment in New York City. The couple's last stop was Shake Shack at Kennedy International Airport, but the customers tweeted that they might not make it since they were running late. What's a Shake Shack employee to do? Well obviously one of them ran some burgers and shakes straight to the gate!

Hospitality-guru Danny Meyer of USHG, the parent company of Gramercy Tavern, Shake Shack, the Modern, and Union Square Cafe, is all about using technology to maintain the personal touch he is famous for in his restaurants. His methods run the gamut from real-time tweets to tightly orchestrated performances coordinated by the Apple Watch. When I spoke with him about his overarching philosophy, he made it clear that in this time when it is so easy to find oneself spending the day in front of screens being a "human doing" instead of a "human being," his goal is to "use tech to enhance touch." To Meyer, this means listening to the conversations his guests are having, both in the restaurant and on social media, and creating (and honoring!) real relationships.

Meyer's Union Square Cafe, the *pièce de résistance* of his USHG brand, recently reopened after a full-scale renovation. Not only has the physical space been updated, but so has the way things get done, including the role of technology, which Danny Meyer has strong feelings about. Technology, he believes, needs to fuel the customer experience and not detract from it. Meyer insists on finding the sweet spot. Guests at Union Square Cafe's new dining room will have to look closely to notice something new on the wrists of certain employees: Apple Watches. While servers won't be using them to input orders (Meyer believes that would create too much of a distraction—a sour spot, if you will), Apple Watches are intended to improve communication on the floor.

Specifically, sommeliers and floor managers wear the device to communicate important information. A manager, for instance, can alert the hostess that a table is ready for the next guests or warn the coatroom that a table has paid its check so the coats should be readied. The sommelier communicates when a bottle of wine has been ordered, so it can be pulled from the cellar ASAP. Saving time improves the customer experience and, of course, the bottom line.[?]

What could be sweeter?

Sweetgreen Makes It Personal

Sweetgreen, the delicious and transparently well-sourced slow fast-food restaurant that's taking over with 75 locations in eight states, knows a thing or two when it comes to balancing technology with human interaction.

In order to keep their customers coming back, Sweetgreen cofounders Nathaniel Ru, Jonathan Neman, and Nicolas Jammet have an interesting angle. They use technology to create what they call "intimacy to scale." What does that mean? It means offering that personalized, *intimate*, "Cheers"-like experience we all appreciate when we walk into a bar, a restaurant, or even up to a counter surrounded by people. The Sweetgreen team wants to bring a personal, sweet spot experience to many, and they embrace technology to do so.

The very notion of "scaling intimacy" might sound oxymoronic and maybe a bit ambitious. However it makes sense in light of Sweetgreen's goal to make customers feel that they aren't just going to any ol' Sweetgreen in the chain, but rather they're going to *their* Sweetgreen. The company achieves this by keeping track of customer preferences, so that every time someone orders a salad, for instance, the person behind the register can remind the customer of past preferences. Sweetgreen has also moved from an assembly line approach to one where an individual employee makes the entire salad, making the Sweetgreen customer experience a little cozier and a little more human.

The Sweetgreen app also aims to create that easy, approachable neighborhood feel by retaining preferences while it facilitates both preordering and payment. Because this is so integral to the company's overall strategy, Sweetgreen invested significant resources into app design, concluding that "the best technology makes life more efficient so you can spend your time actually connecting."[3]

All in all, while "intimacy," "scale," and "technology" might not seem to go together as well as organic baby spinach, warm quinoa, and hot chickpeas, Sweetgreen's numbers—the last reported revenue projections topped $75 million in 2015, back when they had just 39 stores—make it pretty clear that, actually, it's a pretty darn winning combination.[4]

Using technology wisely, just as these masters of hospitality have figured out how to do, allows companies to serve more customers and clients without losing touch with what people are most hungry for—connection.

Fashion Connection Through Tech

Finding that sweet spot is a surefire way to make use of exciting technological advances and take full advantage of what we humans do best—connect with one another. This approach might seem like an obvious fit in some industries and less so in others. But take heed: technology's reach is vast. I can't think of a single business space that wouldn't benefit from thinking about their work in this way. Even something as personal as fashion can bring tech into the mix.

If the Bra Fits, Buy It: ThirdLove Saves the Day

What can I say? Buying bras is a nightmare! The bra is one of the most personal articles of clothing a woman wears, affecting the way everything else looks, fits, and, most importantly, feels. Yet the process is draconian. Surely something less than personal. For those of you who have not had the pleasure, allow me to explain.

You squeeze into a stuffy little room with the most terribly unflattering lights, and maybe a kindly female expert helps you squeeze into typically horribly fitting, horrible-feeling bras. You wrestle with a jillion little plastic hangers, struggling to untangle all the straps. Blood pressure mounts.

Since you're eager to get out of your dressing room, and fast, you choose the least offensive bras you can find. Then, the world evidently adds insult to injury—each bra costs a small fortune! After the cost of the massage and facial you need to de-stress after the experience, you head home feeling ripped off and depressed. Moreover, your bras barely fit.

Enter ThirdLove, an online bra company that brings all the right kinds of intimacy to the bra-buying experience as it replaces the horror and the awkwardness with privacy and noteworthy customer service. Here's the best part: the bras are incredibly comfortable, well fitting, and less expensive than those of many of their competitors.

So how do they do it? With a perfect marriage of tech and connect, that's how.

Heidi Zak cofounded ThirdLove with her husband, Dave Spector. They opened their virtual doors in 2013 and have since attracted a star-studded list of investors, including the ex-CEOs of Victoria's Secret and Spanx. When I chatted with Zak, she told me that she started ThirdLove because, "like a lot of women, [she] really disliked bra shopping." After graduating from the Sloan School of Management at MIT, she "saw a need for something." "It was a category I literally dreaded shopping for," she explained, "I would look and my bra would be ratty . . . stretched out. . . . I really, really, needed to buy new bras, and I really didn't want to have to go to the store."

In 2016, Zak introduced the ThirdLove Fit Finder, a series of online questions relating to a woman's current bra experience—what works, what doesn't—and aiming to determine the exact shape of each customer's breasts. Because ThirdLove has received such "a massive amount of customer data" (approximately 8 million women's fits, amounting to 150 million fit insights[5]), their algorithms can recommend bras with the wisdom and nuance of a "70-year-old bra fitter who's been fitting bras for 50 years."

ThirdLove takes it one step further. Not only does Third-Love offer their customers a bra that fits, the company's high-tech shopping software is also paying such close attention to what each woman likes that personalized recommendations on style and size are a seamless part of the shopping experience. The ThirdLove website makes it clear: "That's the best kind of technology—you don't think about it; you use it because it makes your life easier."

Yep. It seems like they've identified the sweet spot.

However, nothing's perfect, not even the most well-designed product line. When there's a problem with any experience at ThirdLove, Zak has a trained team of 125 female customer-service representatives sitting together in California, at the ready to address concerns. This team of professional, under-standing women is a big investment (each member receives a month of paid, on-the-job training), but it is absolutely essential to ThirdLove's success.

ThirdLove understands that even though the typical in-person bra-buying expedition is pretty painful, perversely there's a lot to be said for the old-school personal attention of an intimate expert. Zak's sweet spot strategy, incorporating an always available human "presence," ensures that her customers won't miss the dressing room.

Maybe she'll even put those dressing-room lightbulb makers out of business.

Smart Mirror, Smart Mirror on the Wall: Rebecca Minkoff's Sweet Spot Tsunami

Millennial fashion designer Rebecca Minkoff, CEO of her eponymously named company, was one of the first to engage customers via social media. She began using Twitter in 2008 and Snapchat in 2013, embracing a new way of honoring cus-tomer relationships both directly and intimately. The impact was so big that the company coined a name for its follow-ers—the "Minkettes." Today there are 800,000 Minkettes on Instagram and 900,000 on Twitter.

When I asked Minkoff about her experience building her brand, she told me, "When I first started the company, I'd communicate with my customers through Twitter. I'd listen to their feedback on the product—what they liked and what they didn't like—and I'd keep it in mind when designing." Technology played such a critical role in the evolution of Rebecca Minkoff the brand, but Minkoff insists that she does not "believe in using technology for technology's sake."[6] Instead, she and so many smart leaders leverage what's great about technology to expand their reach and connect personally with their fans.

Rebecca Minkoff truly lives the sweet spot. Her brand is equal parts "downtown romantic" and "store of the future." With this particular sweet spot in mind, Minkoff is innovating like crazy.

How so? One of Minkoff's most significant contributions to the fashion scene today is her smart dressing room. This room, through the integration of thoughtful technology, creates a more intimate and personal shopping experience. From the beginning, Minkoff has wanted her customers to feel that she herself is really listening to them. She wants them to know that she understands their pain points from the brick-and-mortar shopping environment. This starts with a smart mirror. With a gentle touch on the mirror, you can first place a drink order, making you feel very fancy and pampered. Then you can choose to learn what else Minkoff thinks you might like. This happens through the wizardry of radio frequency identification tags embedded in each piece of clothing. The tags on the clothing you have already chosen are paired with others of Minkoff's choosing. A new take on the personal shopper, this technology allows the Minkette to feel as though Minkoff is just another girlfriend, in the dressing room with her.

The Minkette girlfriend experience doesn't stop there. Let's say, for example, that you find the perfect sundress, but the day and the dressing room are dark and dreary and you can't envision how your new dress will look with the sun beaming down on it during your upcoming trip to Cabo. Just change the lighting! In these smart dressing rooms, customers can adjust the lighting to match the time of day and the setting in which they plan to wear the item.

I'll be honest. When I first heard about Minkoff's new dressing rooms, and visited one myself, I was really impressed. But the real test is whether or not this tech edge will actually influence business.

Well, the results are in. Since launching the mirrors, after combining tech and connect in her boutiques, sales are up 200 percent. That's a veritable sweet spot tsunami!

Whether you're flying passengers though the skies, tending to customers in a restaurant, fashioning a branded clothing empire, or launching any other kind of business, it may take some time to find your sweet spot. But this sort of human effort will be worth it. As Danny Meyer said to me, "Even more than the ROI, it's the return-on-your mission [that matters most], because if your mission is to create more hospitality because it makes people feel better, then that, in and of itself, feeds you."

Taking Meyer's cue, we all need to be fed. We all crave connection. Just remember, technology, when used correctly, can be a great tool for our work lives, but a major hindrance to our personal relationships, if used incorrectly. Use it wisely because finding that sweet spot is good for us as people, great for our businesses, and just might change the world.

SPOTLIGHT

100 Percent Human at Unilever:
An Email-Free CHRO

Leena Nair, Unilever's chief human resources officer, walks the walk when it comes to creating a human workplace. She believes that "[at] the end of the day it's human creativity, empathy, and innovation that takes the world forward."[7] This explains why Nair neither looks at her phone nor responds to *any* emails during the workday. Instead, she gives "100 percent of herself" to her employees. She says, "I don't want to spend my time when I'm at work doing things that I can do by myself later in the day."[8] People now know that she won't respond to email, so if someone needs to reach her, they call or ask her assistant to find her.

Imagine! No email all day?! How sweet it would be!

🤝 HUMAN ACTION PLAN

Finding the sweet spot between tech and connect is a challenge. Honoring relationships is the key. Here are three ways to do that.

1. **Prioritize relationships.** Anyone can say, "Yes, I prioritize relationships." But are you actually putting your money where your mouth is? Ask yourself: Does my calendar reflect my values? How am I spending my time? Have I had lunch with a colleague in the last week or the last month? Am I calling into meetings from down the hall?

   Over the next month, track how you are spending your time and with whom you are spending it.

2. **Position technology.** The key to finding the sweet spot is to position technology so that it strengthens relationships. In other words, match the message to the medium. Identify your goal and think about the best mode of communication to get your message across. Send an email when you need an answer to something without much nuance, but move up the food chain and pick up the phone or walk down the hall if you need to ask someone's opinion, do some real problem solving, or just want to connect with someone you haven't seen in a while.

3. **Establish protocols.** To truly find the sweet spot and implement it in your company's values you must

put protocols in place. Technology allows you to automate parts of your business and reallocate those resources to enhance the customer experience. It's important to help employees understand how to best use technology. Remember Danny Meyer's restaurants and how his floor managers and sommeliers use Apple Watches to communicate with the wait staff? It's up to you to develop the protocols that will help you and your employees get there faster and more effectively. Think about your company's mission and the day-to-day tasks of your employees. Which of these tasks could be automated with technology? Which of these tasks requires a human touch? Then work on a plan to find the sweet spot between tech and connect.

Mind Your Meetings: Honoring Relationships with Purpose, Presence, and Protocols

Every day in the United States, at least 36 million meetings are held.[1] It's no surprise to anyone that, in many of these meetings, people bring in unrelated work, produce grade-school-worthy doodles, and even catch up on some ZZZs. Each year, we waste an estimated $37 billion on unproductive meetings,[2] with executives spending up to 23 hours of their work week in meetings.[3]

For anyone following the meetings-mania coverage of late, none of this will come as a surprise. It is interesting to note, however, that most people still believe that meetings are fruitful, and they don't want to give them up.[4] After all, humans do love to connect. This means that the problem might not be with the number or length of meetings, but rather with the fact that most meetings don't respect people's time, leaving them feeling fatigued, and worse still, abused. All too often, our meetings don't honor relationships.

To make matters still more complicated, according to *Fast Company*, half of all workplaces could be remote by as early as 2020.[5] That doesn't leave us a lot of time to prepare. Whether our meetings are in person or remote, we absolutely must mind them, and mind them well. Meetings, almost by definition, are our opportunities to make those connections that are good for people and great for business.

Have a Purpose

How many times have you and your team reached an impasse on a project and decided that the best way to address the impasse was to have a meeting? Then, someone sends out an invite, and everyone shows up with the problem still on the table, suggesting that simply by virtue of being together you will know what to do next.

Try this: Before sending that invite, pause and ask: "Is this meeting really necessary? If so, what is its purpose?"

Like everything else in the human workplace, meetings are most useful when they are linked directly to a company's values, which then trickle down into preferences and ways of working. If your company values a meticulous process over quick and dirty decision-making, then schedule think-tank-type gatherings periodically, and let go of the more aimless status meetings. Aria Finger, CEO of DoSomething.org, a nonprofit that connects millennials and Gen Z with opportunities to do good in the world, makes "walk and talk" dates with her employees so she can catch up on business *and* get closer to her goal of 10,000 steps a day. If you, like

Finger, prefer to shoot from the hip, then meet standing up or on the go when you have a specific problem that needs hashing out.

A company's meetings and meeting style should reflect its values like everything else it does. Know who you are, and design your meetings accordingly.

SPOTLIGHT

Create Conditions for Creativity

Piera Gelardi is the cofounder and creative genius behind Refinery29, the super stylish and smart online community for women. Once or twice a month, Gelardi hosts a creative brainstorm in her office. Her office is called the Peach Pit because of its peach-colored walls. Why does she host this meeting, in this particular setting? Because, as Gelardi told me, "You have to create the conditions for creativity."

During the meeting, employees are invited to drink rosé, eat peach-flavored candies, and take advantage of a "no limits" buzzer to make sure no idea gets left behind. Gelardi looks for ways to make everyone feel relaxed and welcome to contribute, even those who don't necessarily think of themselves as "creative."

By the looks of the Refinery29's global platform, it's hard to imagine that there is anyone in that company who's not creative! I guess the conditions are ripe.

Tiffany Pham's Values-Driven Meetings

Tiffany Pham is the CEO of the digital powerhouse platform Mogul, reaching 18 million millennial women in 196 countries every week with engaging content. She is a real pro at bringing her company's values to life, and her meetings are no exception.

Pham uses meetings as a way to express and reinforce her company's values among her 50 employees. For example, one of Mogul's values is transparency, something Pham feels is important to show instead of just tell. At every major meeting, Pham shares the company's financials and how Mogul is faring in all of its key metrics. She believes (and I agree with her) that people will only have confidence that an organization is truly transparent if its windows are consistently opened. Meetings are a perfect opportunity to do just that.

A second Mogul value is shared voice. Just as the Mogul platform was developed for users to have a voice, Pham wanted to create a culture in which people at her firm could and would regularly speak up. What better way than in meetings? At Mogul, this means that Pham might ask for an opinion from someone who hasn't spoken up in a while or structure a meeting where everyone is asked to give his or her thoughts.

A third Mogul value that influences meeting culture is education. This is not just for the Mogul audience, but for employees at all levels of the organization. Pham says, "I regularly walk around the office and ask employees in each department how I can support them. . . . In this way, education flows throughout our organization as I further connect and bond, with everyone from our executives to our interns." Pham also meets with her leadership team each week to "gain a sense of what further tools and software might enhance their professional skill sets for their current roles and beyond." Again, this open communication alerts Pham to who needs what, when they need it, and why.

Valuing education means that Pham is always learning, too—about the business and about her employees. At a recent meeting, Pham discovered that one of Mogul's Content and Community team members loves improv. Instead of just nodding and smiling, she heard that this employee was telling her she had an interest in something that might be additive, and she figured out a way to incorporate it into Mogul's future content, which I, for one, can't wait to see. This is a perfect example of the kind of dynamic engagement people want at work. Just because all of Pham's meetings are values-driven doesn't mean that they are all alike. Quite the contrary. Pham is always intentional, but she is also flexible in terms of the form her meetings take. She holds a range of meetings, from formal end-of-week wrap-ups that are also celebrations (called "Weekly Wins") to informal, personal check-ins and regularly scheduled status updates. Pham respects the power of values-driven meetings in every shape and size.

Pham's nimble approach to meetings is uncommon and impressive. Pham walks the walk and her people feel heard.

Remember, values-driven doesn't mean cookie-cutter, but rather that these values are woven into the context of each meeting. Meetings should be a way to connect and share in the communal culture that you and your employees love.

SPOTLIGHT

Find Your Center

Karan Rai, the CEO of Asgard Partners & Co., is a deep believer in process, and he is dedicated to helping his employees be their best selves. One way he does this is through his weekly partners meeting, which, according to Rai, "is the one meeting each week that no one misses."

Every Tuesday morning, Rai calls together his senior partners for a meeting where no "official" business gets done. Instead, the purpose of the meeting is to go through a process that "brings his people back to center" and helps them remember who they aspire to be. To do this, the partners read their personal mission statements every week. "The way I look at it, if I can keep the leaders in my company living on purpose, I have a much higher probability of building a company that is truly purpose driven, which gives my company the best chance of long term and sustainable success," he explains.[6]

Be Present

As Randi Zuckerberg, CEO of Zuckerberg Media and author of *Dot Complicated and Pick Three*, explains, "Your presence is no longer a sign that you're actually paying attention."

Isn't that the truth?

When I worked with MIT professor Sherry Turkle, author of *Reclaiming Conversation*, we talked a lot about a phenomenon that she refers to as "phubbing," otherwise known as "phone snubbing."[7] She writes, "College students tell me they know how to look someone in the eye and type on their phones at the same time, their split attention undetected. They say it's a skill they mastered in middle school when they wanted to text in class without getting caught. Now they use it when they want to be both with their friends and, as some put it, 'elsewhere.'"[8]

College students aren't the only ones splitting their attention. Multitasking in the workplace is a serious and costly epidemic. Research out of Workplace Options discovered that social media distractions may cost the U.S. economy $650 billion per year.[9] Our meetings are a breeding ground for multitasking.

We've all been there. Colleagues sit around the table at a meeting presenting their findings on a project. More often than not, people are surreptitiously texting under the table, scrolling through their email, or perusing their Instagram feed, all while maintaining eye contact. Not only is the "Wait, what?" response very rude, it's also bad for business and for our brains! Research has shown, time and time again, that multitasking erodes productivity and results.[10]

So if meetings are that tricky, why bother? This is a question many people are asking and rightly so. We have witnessed the enormous amount of time lost and the resentment gained from all these meetings. On the other hand, we have also observed that people like to meet. If you take the plunge and send out that invite, first and foremost, make sure the meeting has a purpose. Then, insist that everyone invited makes his or her presence known. When you call people together, it's up to you to honor the relationships you aim to build.

Set the Tone—Literally

Let's face it. Whatever compelling piece of business is on our agenda, we are competing with infinite distractions. To ensure we are present from the very beginning of each and every meeting, we must set the tone.

Sometimes this means we ring an actual bell. This is what fashion maverick Eileen Fisher does. She opens her meetings with the chime of a meditation gong, indicating that it's time for a centering moment of quiet. Sometimes it means setting the tone the way Microsoft CEO Satya Nadella does. He opens his senior leadership meetings with what is called "Researcher of the Amazing," a story from one executive (a seat that rotates each month) on how some piece of Microsoft technology is being used in alignment with Microsoft values. One example described Microsoft engineers in Turkey connecting through video conference to reveal an app they developed for reading books aloud to the visually impaired.[11] It can also mean bringing people together the way Lyft does. The ride-sharing start-up asks new hires for a few fun facts that can be used in a light roast at their first all-hands meeting.

Because here's the thing: left to our own devices, we are just not connecting. While we used to be able to just get a bunch of people together in a room and watch the connection sparks fly, these days there is so much competing for our attention that we must be more intentional. When it comes to meetings, like it or not, we must curate connection and add a little cruise director to our manager mentality.

One New York City–based financial services firm captured its employees' attention by hiring a professional journalist to come and interview their top executives. This ultimately proved to be an entertaining way of humanizing the bosses and definitely got everyone's attention. At Zendesk, a powerhouse company that builds customer service software for giants such as Slack, they change up their happy hour by getting their execs behind the bar mixing drinks, regardless of whether or not they've ever previously poured a cocktail.[12] I love this idea. "Turning the tables" gets employees' attention, everyone has a few laughs at the leaders' expense, and it's a creative way to encourage employees to be present.

You don't have to hire a magician to grab your employees' attention. Even simple efforts and little tweaks work too. Centro, a digital advertising firm in Chicago, begins each meeting with a simple round-robin check-in, asking each participant to share a bit about how she or he is feeling. This allows people to be present by addressing where they are emotionally as well as physically.

To counter meeting doldrums, workplace strategist Max Chopovsky suggests that people use physical space to improve their meetings. Chopovsky recommends "reduc[ing] the number of long and narrow conference room tables, to create a more collaborative environment and encourage inclusive conversation."[13] Conference rooms should instead be furnished with circular tables, which create a more inclusive and open dynamic that allows for better interaction and communication. Remember King Arthur's Knights of the Round Table? According to legend, the great king valued his knights' input and frequently sat down with them to discuss strategies at a circular table, and Camelot was stronger because of it. Perhaps the King of Camelot was on to something! On a personal note, this fix is especially resonant to me: whenever I go out to dinner with a group, I always request a circular table to improve the conversation dynamics.

Setting the tone for diversity in meetings means making sure we don't just bring people to the table, but that we hear from them and listen to them as well. Meetings are notoriously dominated by a few very comfortable speakers. Kellogg School of Management Professor Leigh Thompson's research tells us that two people typically do more than 60 percent of the talking in a six-person meeting. If the group size is increased, the issue is exacerbated.[14] Even if we manage to assemble truly diverse teams (empirically the most effective), it stands to reason that they won't do us much good if we don't hear from everyone who is present.

Adam Grant, prolific author and Wharton professor, urges people to be on the lookout for meeting conformity. He suggests that the leader of any meeting should consider herself the welcoming committee, making eye contact and even calling on people. That leader might also consider being the last to speak. Susan Cain, author of *Quiet*, agrees and says that introverts actually appreciate being called on. At the same time, she also recommends that introverts "prepare their thoughts ahead of time," doing whatever they need to do to feel comfortable speaking up.[15]

Think back to your last meeting. What happened? Was it a wide-ranging, nonconformist exploration of the topic at hand? Or did all attendees keep their comments brief and tentative, waiting for the person "in charge" to chime in and then return to the same old symphony of "what she said"? If the latter, an email may have done the trick. You and your company deserve better.

Create Protocols

Okay. Your meeting has a purpose, and you have established some encouraging pathways to presence. Then in the middle of the meeting a phone rings, gradually people's attention gravitates toward their laps, and one by one, phones, iPads, and computers come out, while everyone remarkably continues to maintain eye contact. Even with the best intentions, you're getting phubbed in your own meeting.

Rest assured, this scenario is happening in conference rooms all around the country, not just yours. It seems like this technology has been around forever, but the truth is that it's all brand new, and we have no idea how to use it (think George Jetson on a treadmill . . . *get me off this crazy thing!*). When I am in offices, I often feel like it's the Wild West, with all these tones and beeps and rings and pings, and we need to establish some order around here. If you happen to be the one charged with creating that order, it's up to you to develop rules of the road and make them stick. If you are not in such a position but nonetheless feel the need for some order, by all means say something! You won't be the only one.

The good news is that there are many ways to set protocols for a meeting. You can send a checklist of "pre-work" to give the meeting context. You can send a clear agenda, with enough advance notice for everyone to read and reflect upon it before the meeting, which is a great way to engage introverts. You can also assign someone to keep time against an agenda, making sure the meeting stays on task. Other protocol tricks include placing a basket outside the conference room for all devices or only allowing attendees to use devices for the last few minutes of a meeting to schedule the follow-up.

Here are some inspiring case studies that show how some smart humans manage to set meeting protocols to honor relationships.

Values Are LinkedIn to Meetings
for Jeff Weiner

Jeff Weiner, the popular CEO of LinkedIn, is perhaps best known for his emphasis on what he calls compassionate management, a practice of protocols inspired by the Dalai Lama's book *The Art of Happiness*. Weiner writes, "I learned the difference between compassion, defined as walking a mile in another person's shoes, and empathy, which is feeling what another person feels."[16] It's this aspiration to understand where people are coming from (he admits that he hasn't conquered compassion) that lies at the heart of his management style. Weiner and LinkedIn, by the way, have seen through-the-roof success, with revenues growing from $78 million to over $4 billion in just a few years and an acquisition by Microsoft for more than $26 billion.[17]

Nowadays, all-hands and town hall meetings are *de rigueur* for nearly every company, large and small. Just as pervasive is a belief that such meetings are kind of dull, predictable, and not really worth the time of those at the top. However, this isn't the case at LinkedIn, given how Weiner runs his show. LinkedIn's all-hands meeting is held every other Wednesday at 10 a.m., usually out of its Sunnyvale, California headquarters. Every senior leader on Weiner's team of nine, as well as more than 60 vice presidents, all typically attend. LinkedIn's more than 11,000 employees join in person, stream at their offices around the globe, or watch the replays with their teams. Even more impressive, Jeff Weiner himself runs the meeting.

For a CEO of a major company to attend, let alone lead, a biweekly town hall meeting is unusual to say the least. This speaks volumes about the values of the person who does. Weiner is like a good old-fashioned mail carrier, leading his meeting in rain, sleet, snow, and hail. Such a commitment to an all-hands meeting is a powerful demonstration of LinkedIn's culture and values in action. When this meeting was at one point broadcast from San Francisco instead of its usual Sunnyvale home, there was a line of people waiting to get in. Everyone knows these meetings are not box-checking exercises. Quite the opposite. Real information is conveyed in real time, and anyone who wants to be in the know will attend and respect whatever is shared. There's a saying at LinkedIn that "what happens at the all-hands stays at the all-hands," and that mutual trust allows incredible candor and transparency.

One of LinkedIn's values is *relationships matter*, and Weiner is determined to honor and invest in those relationships. Every other Wednesday at 10 a.m.

An Invitation to Be Heard at Netflix

Todd Yellin is a senior vice president of product strategy at Netflix. Like Jeff Weiner, Yellin is hell-bent on making meetings valuable, but his approach is very different. Honoring relationships and accomplishing real work is so important that Yellin leaves nothing to chance. In Todd Yellin's universe, protocols are king.

The way Yellin runs his weekly product strategy meeting is so truly inspiring that some of his Netflix colleagues have been implementing these ideas in their own meetings. His meetings always abide by one cardinal rule: *If you're coming to the meeting, you must be there, in body and mind.* That means, you guessed it, absolutely no technology.

So who comes to this product strategy meeting given that no one is required to attend? Lots of people. Between 15 to 50 people usually attend, depending on the topic. One of the most amazing things about Yellin's meetings is that, as exciting and high level as they are (imagine the fun of talking product strategy at Netflix!), Yellin really strives to democratize the meeting process. Yellin shared with me that all Netflix employees are welcome, but there will be no "peanut galleries." If anyone from the company wants to attend, they just have to do two simple things: be prepared and contribute. No sitting around.

What does it mean to "be prepared" for one of Yellin's meetings? It means reading the detailed pre-meeting memo in Google Docs before arrival (and remember, there's no technology, so there won't be any scrolling through as the meeting gets started). It means adding comments and questions directly on the document, if you so choose. If all you want to do is offer your two cents virtually, through your comments, and skip the meeting altogether, that works for Yellin, too.

Because Yellin is so determined to get feedback from all types of folks, not just the extroverts, he's moved away from what he described to me as the "Jeopardy" style of meetings, where everyone just waits to hit the proverbial buzzer with the right answer. Instead, he has people raise their hands in meetings, and they take turns.

That's not all though. I think my very favorite part of Yellin's meeting style is how he explicitly tells people to attend only the parts of the meeting that are relevant to them. He knows full well how unproductive it is for busy people to sit in a meeting that has nothing to do with them and space out (since they can't text under the table). Forcing people to sit through meetings is a waste of precious time and no way to honor relationships.

So, as part of his protocol setting, Yellin says, if you aren't literally and figuratively present, stay away. Period. Now, that's clarity!

When I asked Yellin how his rules of the road were being received, he said that people are really positive, noting that without technology, everyone seems to feel the meetings are more efficient and more substantive. The people in the meeting are engaged and ready to add value.

As Elmar Nubbemeyer, a relatively new Netflix employee, informed me, "What makes Todd's setup more human [than other companies where I have worked] is it gives the freedom for you to be listened to without making a lot of fuss. You don't need to bring a slide. You don't need to think very hard about how you are going to express yourself. You can do it in the comments. You can do it live. But you are getting heard. And that is something I appreciate."

One of the best parts of writing this book has been seeing just how true it is that there is no one-size-fits-all approach for anything. Todd Yellin honors relationships by making sure people respect each other and their own time. Jeff Weiner honors relationships by giving people permission to schedule their work and their lives around a meaningful, companywide meeting.

Both approaches work. Because both allow employees to bring their human to work.

SPOTLIGHT

The 30-Minute Meeting

Because nobody should spend all day in meetings, Barri Rafferty, CEO of Ketchum PR, has made it a rule that people can only book meetings for 30 minutes or less. If an employee needs longer, he has to make a special request (which not many people end up doing). The 30-minute rule forces the person requesting the meeting to come very prepared and ready to get to the heart of the issue.

Rafferty is also trying out a concept she calls "outcome-based" meetings, where instead of attending three meetings with three groups on a specific issue, she meets with all three groups at one time. The collaborative meeting approach enables people to learn from each other and connect the dots themselves on the cross-functional issues.

And she gets to attend one meeting instead of three.

PS: Remote Meetings Are Virtually the Same as In-Person Meetings, with One Big Difference

A respectful meeting that honors relationships can happen in person or remotely, and both types require the same three ingredients for success: purpose, presence, and protocols. The one big difference for remote meetings is that before you can set any of these three ingredients, the meeting platform—Skype, Zoom, Google Hangout, or any of the many available options—must be taught and understood by all meeting attendees. Imagine an in-person meeting dominated by questions about how to sit in a chair or take turns listening. Until virtual meeting platforms are just as easy as in-person ones, it will be impossible to get much further or deeper than the frustrating cacophony of "I can't hear everyone," "Sorry, I can't see you," and "Darn, you're frozen," that we've all experienced.

For instance, in a weekly staff meeting with her remote team, a Google manager used—what else?—Google Hangout. Her team knew the guidelines for these meetings; they received their agendas ahead of time, and they were encouraged to stand up and hold a cup of coffee to imitate the feeling of a face-to-face meeting. For the record, if you are standing up and holding a cup of coffee, you are less likely to be multitasking on your phone.

Even more importantly for this meeting is that everyone involved knows how to do one important thing that we often take for granted: turn on the camera. Okay, two things. Also know where to look. Don't skip the small stuff!

And Finally, Pause

When we mind our meetings, we practice being purposeful, being present, and instituting protocols. That is to say, we don't mess around with people's time. Therefore, before sending out that meeting invite, take a moment and pause. Ask yourself: "Is this meeting necessary? Were the right people there the last time? What could be changed?"

If you are one of those people who really does need to be in meetings for much of the day, take some advice from Warby Parker CEO Dave Gilboa. Gilboa manages to reflect purposefully on his many meetings, rating them (each week) a zero, one, or two. "Zero means it was a really bad use of time, and if I had to do it again, I wouldn't have attended that meeting at all. Two is a great use of time—I want to spend more of my time in those types of meetings. And one is somewhere in-between."[18] Then, he shares his thoughts with his assistant, who helps manages his calendar, and together they come up with a solid meeting strategy.

It's not surprising that one of Warby Parker's values is learn, grow, repeat. Clearly, this successful founder's meetings reflect those values.

I'll admit it. I love a good meeting! From a human point of view, intentional face-to-face interaction is like gold. We just have to learn how to mine for it by running each one through a human test: Does it have purpose, presence, and protocols? If so, it's a keeper.

HUMAN ACTION PLAN

How to Mind Your Meetings

1. **Know the purpose.** Before you attend or plan a meeting, ask yourself: What is the meeting's purpose? And is that purpose aligned with your goals and objectives or those of your team? I recently came across a great story about a company that asks its employees to choose one meeting each week to decline. This thought process forces people to continually evaluate the relevance of their meetings—and to be thinking "Is this the one I should decline?"

   You should ask yourself the following questions: Which meetings in your schedule could be handled without calling a meeting on the mound? How many of your meetings this week were productive?

   Before each meeting create an agenda that outlines the purpose of the meeting and the goals you hope to accomplish at the end.

2. **Be present.** Physical and mental presence are not the same. So, if you decide to attend a meeting, be there in mind, body, and spirit. If you are leading the meeting, make sure your team does the same. Why? Because it's good for business. When you have a room full of people saying, "Wait, what?" productivity goes down, and time is wasted. When an employee is presenting something to the group, and her colleagues are texting under the table, it hurts relationships.

Design your meetings so that employees who attend are required to engage. Find ways to encourage employees to speak up and voice their opinions. Literally set the tone for the meeting. Start the meeting with an icebreaker by asking attendees to each share an interesting fact about themselves. Because true presence is a critical way to honor relationships.

3. **Set protocols.** It's such an important topic that it bears repeating: without protocols, meetings do not serve their purpose, and that's why we're here in the first place! The protocols used by Tiffany Pham, Jeff Weiner, and Todd Yellin may not feel right for your organization. That's fine. Pick ones that feel right to you and are aligned with your values and culture. Whether you choose to ban technology or set strict regulations for meeting lengths and frequency, be sure to communicate these protocols to your team.

   You can even solicit ideas from team members and involve them in the process. Ask your team-mates to provide feedback about recent meetings. Ask them what worked and what didn't work, and establish meeting protocols based on the feedback.

5

Well-Being at Work: Finding the Human Side of Wellness

When Italian physician Bernardino Ramazzini encountered a cesspool operator with an eye infection, he had an "aha" moment. He recognized that there is a connection between what we do for a living and our health. An important revelation, indeed! Ramazzini went on to write *A Treatise on the Diseases of Tradesmen,* signaling the founding of occupational medicine in the Western world in 1700,[1,2] and, arguably, the dawn of the corporate wellness program.

Today, 70 percent of U.S. employers offer some kind of wellness program.[3] The so-called wellness industry itself is pretty healthy, humming along to the tune of $8 billion a year.[4]

The typical motivation behind these programs is not a mystery. When an employer pays for its workforce's health insurance, an individual's health becomes a matter of self-interest. Even when insurance premiums are not paid for, wellness programs are often thought to be good for the bottom line. One oft-cited study by well-known cardiologists Richard Milani and Carl Lavie offered a pretty basic wellness program to employees and found that "every dollar invested in the intervention yielded $6 in healthcare savings."[5]

It's not difficult to make the argument that providing a path to wellness is just plain human. As a 2015 report by the nonprofit Health Enhancement Research Organization (HERO) makes clear, there is much to be gained by a more human approach to wellness in our work lives. The HERO authors write that while "senior business leaders turn to workforce [wellness] initiatives in an effort to control healthcare costs," there is much to be said for a "broader value proposition such as increased productivity and performance, higher engagement and morale, and lower turnover rates."[6]

For instance, *Harvard Business Review* reports on a study of organizations with highly effective wellness programs. These organizations have a 9 percent turnover rate, while organizations with ineffective programs have a 15 percent turnover rate.[7]

What does it mean to have a "highly effective" wellness program? The authors of the HERO study believe such programs focus on "social, financial, spiritual, and mental wellbeing."

That is to say, since we're bringing our human to work, our whole human selves need to be kept in check, not just our cholesterol.

More and more companies are trending toward holistic wellness programs that go above and beyond the treadmill-pushing programs of the past to include standing desks, financial fluency, mental health support, and mindfulness.[8] At the heart of these programs is not just "health," but broad well-being, making the human "being" a focus of wellness.

It's hard to fill all the buckets of genuine well-being. So, I've approached this chapter differently. Instead of giving examples of a wide range of companies with a great take on designing the human workplace, I offer a case study of one exemplary company that personifies well-being in everything it does—in its mission, its values, and its own wellness. The company, Vynamic, is a Philadelphia-based consulting firm that specializes in healthcare. The goal of its CEO, Dan Calista, is to build the healthiest company in the world.

And judging from what I've seen, he's right on track.

Vynamic: A Case Study

Janet Binswanger is an outgoing, friendly mother of two with decades of experience in the hospitality industry. When she lost her job with a catering company, she reached out to the CEO at one of her corporate connections, asking if he happened to know of anyone who might need an in-house hospitality specialist. At first Dan Calista, founder and CEO of Vynamic, said he was so sorry, but no.

The next day, Calista reconsidered and called Binswanger back to say that, actually, there was a maternity leave opening that might be just right for her within his own consulting shop. That was in 2015. Today, Binswanger is Vynamic's full-time "curator." Her job includes researching the best snacks for employees, keeping tabs on the corporate apartment, and curating special experiences for employees and clients. For the more than 100 employees of a company making headlines for its radical embrace of wellness, this is a critical job. Binswanger gushes, "I'm so happy here. This place is life-changing." Binswanger is not alone. One young consultant named Kristal confessed to me, "If I won the lottery I would come back to Vynamic."

The kind of loyalty and engagement that Calista has inspired is the holy grail of businesses around the world. Many studies show that this kind of devotion doesn't come from high salaries or cash bonuses. While a cool culture helps, a Ping-Pong table does not a happy employee make, especially for millennials in their dogged —and legitimate!—search for meaning. Fun, after all, is great, but it's not enough.[9]

Recognition is also nice, as is time off and a great space, and the other 9 out of 10 practices in this book. But as I have written throughout, there is one ingredient that is key to all of the big efforts to find that special sauce to keep and retain talent and customers, across industries and up and down the food chain. It's simple: we need to honor relationships. By focusing on wellness, Dan Calista demonstrates his commitment to do just that.

With its on-the-go, at-the-ready lifestyle, consulting is one of the most grueling, unhealthy industries. On a plane. Off a plane. One time zone, then another. I should know. This was my life for many years.

A lifelong entrepreneur whose first business was selling party tents, Calista began his consulting career at Accenture, which he called the "Broadway of business." He loved working with such smart and interesting clients, but he did not like the stressful lifestyle. Calista was convinced there was a better way. In 2008, he left Accenture and rolled out "the world's shortest business plan." As Calista explains, it all started with "Vynamic," a word he created to serve as his guide and inspiration.

Vynamic didn't start as a healthcare consultancy. Instead, as Calista shared with me, it started with the "V" in "Vynamic," which stands for "Values and Vitality," and the rest is, of course, "dynamic." With that values-laden, "Vynamic" core and nomenclature in mind, Calista's next step was to decide on a sector for his firm. "I followed the V," he said, which led to "the industry of our generation," a place where "morals and money" come together, a place that gets "really, really messy."

Namely, healthcare presented itself to Calista as an opportunity of a lifetime—he could help people by healing an industry.

Since opening Vynamic's doors, Calista has made it his business not only to support healthcare and right its wrongs, but also to be the "healthiest company in the world and to spread the health." Vynamic aspires to be a place where people are encouraged and expected to take care of themselves and others, a place where employees regard their work as more than a job, but a joy. Most clearly, the Vynamic website says, "Healthy culture is our business strategy."[10]

Calista is one of those people whose mission is so clear and so strong, he can't help but manifest it in everything he does.

The Work: You Don't Have to Work in Kentucky, Unless You Want To

One of Calista's most foundational well-being initiatives is also his most radical. He allows consultants to choose their projects and their locations, instead of the more conventional "go where the job is" and "do what you're told" approach of most (if not all) other consulting firms. This creates a "no-debt environment" for Calista, where consultants need not do their managers any favors by taking on projects they don't want. Being asked to go on such projects can foster resentment and an ingrained focus on payback instead of the goodwill Calista wants among the ranks.

I have to admit that when I first heard about this strategy, I was cynical. In my experience as a consultant, as much as leaders want to give employees like me a choice, at the end of the day if the leadership development project I was working on was based in Kentucky, I was going to be on the next plane to Kentucky. Yet at Vynamic, consultants really do get a vote. They don't have to go to Kentucky if they don't feel like it.

While I was in the Vynamic lunchroom with Calista, talking about this policy, a consultant happened to walk by our table. She had just returned from her second maternity leave and told me a story which exemplifies what makes Vynamic a human workplace. When she returned from her first maternity leave, a senior leader outlined two potential projects she could work on, and they discussed the pros and cons of each one together. Project number one resembled others she had worked on before and could be an easy way to transition back with a new baby. Project number two was in a new area of the business, one with a steeper learning curve, but one in which she had previously expressed interest. The choice was hers. Having this conversation made her feel empowered and allowed her to make a choice that worked for her and her family. She felt cared for at a time when many women and men coming back to work can feel pretty challenged.

By allowing his employees to have a say in choosing their projects, Calista is honoring his most important relationship—the one with his employees—and building kindness into the very fabric of the company. Calista believes this commitment to wellness leads to a more loyal workforce. The data backs him up! Vynamic's attrition rate is 10 percent[11] as compared to between 15 and 20 percent for other comparable consultancies.[12]

In other words, people want to stay! Another plus side is that since employees are working on projects that make them happy, they tell their friends about their amazing job. This opens the door to other quality applicants. At a time when most firms like his are desperate for top talent, Calista hires just 1.4 percent of its qualified applicants,[13] a full 70 percent of which come from employee referrals.[14]

Now, that's well-being at work.

SPOTLIGHT

Fitness, Flex, and Fools

Samantha Whiteside is the "Chief Wellness Fool" at the Motley Fool, an online tool for personal investing. Whiteside's job title alone says something about this firm's commitment to well-being. Being Chief Wellness Fool, Whiteside writes the *Flex*, a monthly health newsletter focusing on a specific wellness theme (for example, April was Active April) and a "wellness fool," someone nominated by peers. Whiteside challenges her employees to choose one meeting per week to be an active one. They can go on a walk together, do push-ups at the meeting, or take a class together.

As Whiteside says, "I'm able to pull 'Fools' from different departments [who] may have had only one conversation before, [and bring them] together to collaborate in a spinning, boot camp, or other kind of fitness class."[17]

At the Motley Fool, collaboration is just another opportunity to be well. Sounds more clever than foolish to me.

And How!: Working Well-Being into the Day-to-Day

About five years ago, Laura Pappas, one of Calista's consultants, approached him about her growing interest in the field of wellness coaching. Sensing an opportunity and wanting to encourage his employee, Calista invited Pappas to pursue that interest and even offered to pay for her to become a Certified Health Coach (CHC).

This is how Vynamic's very own "health and care" position was born.

Having an on-site coordinator of health and care makes it clear to everyone that Calista means business in his commitment to well-being. From healthy snacks to treadmill desks, ergonomically correct chairs, and special LED lights, Pappas now covers all the wellness bases for Vynamic. For consultants who work on-site with local clients, Pappas even arranges for these amenities to be delivered!

As we know, there is more to wellness than taking care of the body. One of Pappas's "health and care" initiatives is called Be Your Best Self. Be Your Best Self is a customized coaching and empowerment program for employees who want to set personal goals—be they financial or emotional—and receive help meeting them.

For instance, if an employee wants to start practicing mindfulness, Pappas will help that person find a good program, pay for an introductory class, and then follow up on a regular basis. But supporting well-being doesn't end there for Vynamic! Other employee goals have included bringing lunch from home (this person received a gift card to Whole Foods), learning calligraphy (this person was offered a workshop), and doing window-box gardening (this person received a credit at Lowe's). We are complicated beings who need artistic expression as much as regular exercise. Calista is smart for encouraging and empowering his employees to strive for truly balanced lives. Recently, Laura Pappas decided she wanted to return to her consulting role. Calista helped transition Pappas back into consulting, and another employee raised her hand to oversee Vynamic's health and care program.

The Vynamic approach to well-being at work is not limited to workstation support and extracurricular empowerment. Employees are also supported through incredibly thoughtful communication scaffolding. One example of this is a regular open forum called "Project Huddle." During each session, a team member from human resources facilitates. He or she asks all employees exploratory questions, such as "What does balance mean to you?" Project Huddle gives people the opportunity to openly share their thoughts and feelings on topics relevant to the ways they work together. Moreover, they get to know each other in the process. Not only does this kind of bonding make people feel good, but study after study shows that being friends with coworkers improves overall performance.[15]

Not surprisingly, Calista's employees rate Vynamic as 98 percent on great challenges, great communication, and great bosses, and 100 percent on great atmosphere and great pride.[16]

Vynamic employs another helpful communication structure called the "Three Amigos." This framework refers to three very different—and very supportive—relationships employees can call upon in different capacities. The Three Amigos are your "go-to," your counselor, and your account manager. While all three serve as potential mentors and coaches, each plays a different role. Your go-to is the person who can answer practical questions about your current project (what many companies would call your supervisor or project manager), your counselor is a person you have chosen as a career mentor, and your account manager is the person who manages the client relationship. Because these relationships are so important, their development is not left to chance. There are very clear guidelines in place for how to communicate. For instance, "30 in 30" for go-tos means that that an employee is expected to spend a minimum of 30 minutes checking-in with his or her go-to every 30 days. Ultimately, all Three Amigos contribute to employees' performance reviews.

So here again, relationships matter at Vynamic. And relationships are key to well-being at work and everything else in this book.

SPOTLIGHT

Mindset Mondays at Deloitte

According to Mike Preston, the chief talent officer at Deloitte, "We are a leadership culture focused on the development of well-being of all of our people. . . . At Deloitte, [millennials are] almost 55 to 60 percent of our population, [and] we have to design systems that will enable us to attract and retain talent." What does this generation want? Well-being! While time off is important, research at Deloitte has found that there are also small things that employees can do to improve well-being. Dr. Kelly Monahan, a subject-matter specialist from Deloitte's Center for Integrated Research shared an experiment that Deloitte did with a group of managers. Managers were asked to set aside 15 minutes a week to focus on their "mindset." This was a time for them to re-center their purpose and check in with themselves.

During these 15 minutes, managers were reminded
to turn off their devices and email and really
focus. Deloitte found that the group that par-
ticipated in the program saw a 20 to 30 percent
increase in employee engagement. This 15 minutes
a week has become what they call Mindset Mon-
day. What a great way to kick off a week![18]

But When? Turn It Off and Catch Some ZZZs

Calista's entrepreneurial wisdom has been good for his company's business. In 2017 Vynamic's revenue was $24.5 million,[19]
placing it in line with similar-sized consultancies,[20] which is
darn impressive. And in July 2017 the company was acquired
by UDG Healthcare. The acquisition, Calista says, "creates tre-
mendous value for our client and the people of Vynamic."[21]

Calista's consultants call Vynamic the "utopia of consulting" because of the healthy guardrails he has established
around his employees' work lives, which cover the "what" and
the "how" of employee well-being. But it's Calista's response
to "When?" that has garnered him the most accolades of all.
In addition to the multitude of Vynamic's professional awards,
including being named one of *Fortune*'s 30 Best Workplaces
for Professional Services, one of America's Best Management
Consulting Firms by *Forbes*, and Ivy Exec's #1 Boutique Consulting Firm, Vynamic and Calista have also been recognized
for one of their most important and influential programs, called
zzzMail.

It's no wonder that "The Today Show," *Harvard Business
Review*, *Time Magazine,* and *Fast Company* (to name a few)
have highlighted this important policy of Calista's. The zzzMail

policy eliminates work emails between the hours of 10 p.m. and 6 a.m. and on the weekends. That's one doozy of a protocol! And don't even think about sending a message right before 10 p.m. or before 6 a.m. If you do, you will be known far and wide as the employee who dropped a "Z-bomb."

If something's ugent, Calista says, "Call or text" to get the person's serious attention and engagement.

It's one thing to go the extra mile and encourage relationship-building within one's own business, but at Vynamic, there's also an uncommonly human element in recognizing that all relationships matter, especially those with our families, friends, and loved ones outside of the office. This is what makes zzzMail so powerful. One consultant said, as a guest on "The Today Show": "It gives you that sense of peace that permeates the rest of your life."

When NBC correspondent Jo Ling Kent asked Calista how this radically human program was affecting the bottom line, Calista confessed, "It actually helps it. That's the crazy secret." When Kent pressed, "By how much?" Calista laughed and countered, "Well, it's long-term sustainability. Every year we grow profits."

And there we have it, folks. The long game wins again.

At Vynamic, well-being includes human schedules. This means that even high performers generally work from 8 a.m. to 4:30 p.m., all employees receive four months of 100-percent paid parental leave, and Vynamic offers multitudes of opportunities to give back and participate in community life. This comes in addition to the just plain great healthcare work the company's smart-as-a-whip consultants are doing to transform what they and Calista consider "the industry of our generation." All in all, Vynamic is a values-driven, wellness-celebrating success story, honoring relationships every step of the way.

Reminder: Be Nice—It's Actually Good for Your Health

Former surgeon general Dr. Vivek H. Murthy made a startling statement in 2016. He declared that the most common disease in America is neither cancer nor heart disease. Rather, it is isolation and social disconnection that afflict most Americans.[22] Murthy also reported that programs that address emotional well-being have a positive impact on employee health and workplace productivity.

So if you feel a little overwhelmed after reading about Vynamic's super-success, or if you simply don't have the bandwidth to launch a fully-baked wellness program, Christine Porath, professor of management at Georgetown University, has great news for you. Author of *Mastering Civility: A Manifesto for the Workplace*, Porath writes about how the "epidemic of rudeness" is responsible for a whole host of health problems. She writes that incivility can deplete our immune system and cause cardiovascular disease, cancer, diabetes, and ulcers.[23] If that weren't evidence enough, a 2012 study by the Harvard School of Public Health concluded that stressful jobs were just as bad for women's health as smoking and obesity.[24] Adding injury to insult, Porath reports, a recent study on civility in a medical setting revealed how just one rude comment negatively affected both diagnostic and procedural performance by up to 52 percent.[25]

Where's the great news? Porath reminds us, simply, that if you're not sure where to start, wonder no more. Just be nice. And make sure your employees are too.

SPOTLIGHT

Solving for Germs

When CBRE, the world's largest commercial real estate and investing firm, began to renovate and repurpose its offices and move to an open-desk system, in which people could switch desks whenever they so chose, one concern was germs. Specifically, who was sitting in the spot before you, and what kind of "cooties" did they have (It turns out that, by coincidence and good fortune, they were making the switch during flu season). This germ issue catalyzed a companywide emphasis on health and wellness.

In their renovation, CBRE solved for germs by using antimicrobial surfaces, increasing janitorial support, and implementing a clean-desk policy for the end of every day. The Los Angeles office became the first building in the country to be WELL-certified, an international recognition of buildings that are good for people (by meeting high standards for quality on parameters such as air, water, nourishment, light, fitness, comfort, and mind[26]). This CBRE office now ensures that healthy snacks and drinking water are readily available. They have also implemented Wellness Wednesdays, when employees benefit from wellness perks such as massage therapists and speakers who discuss nutrition and exercise.

That's taking well-being to heart.

HUMAN ACTION PLAN

The concept of well-being at work is relatively new but growing at a rapid pace. Here are three ways to get your company's well-being off the ground by taking care of the whole humans on your team—body, mind, and spirit.

1. **Design.** Each company is different, so be sure to design a well-being strategy that's right for your company, aligned with what is most important to your company, your employees, and *your values*. Does it make sense to focus on stress reduction? On mindfulness? Do your employees need to connect more to reduce isolation-related depression? Do you need to focus on workplace incivility? Are people sitting at their desks too long? Do they need to get up and moving to hit their 10,000 steps? What does your company need? And how can you best deliver?

   Talk to your employees and ask them what they crave. Once you know what your employees need to feel happy and healthy, design your company's wellness plan around what your team wants.

2. **Communicate.** Once you have designed your well-being program, let employees know that their well-being is important and show them how to take advantage of what your organization has to offer. As always, match the message to the medium, and consider the range of ways to communicate your

commitment. Whether you write a fitness newsletter like the Motley Fool, talk about well-being in a town hall–style meeting, install a dedicated meditation room, or set up a Slack wellness channel, communication is critical. If employees don't know what's available, all your hard work will be lost.

3. **Measure.** You trust that employee well-being is good for people and good for business. But how can you be sure your specific programs are doing the trick for your workforce? In order to measure your ROW (Return on Wellness), put solid metrics in place and make some simple observations. How many people are engaging in the program? Have absences increased or decreased? What are your healthcare costs, pre- and post-program? What does a cross section of your team have to say about the program? Measuring impact is important as it will showcase the benefits to employees themselves. Metrics are also important so you can understand what's working and what isn't and be able to adjust accordingly.

6

Give Back: You've Got Nothing to Lose, Only Inspired Employees to Gain

Fortune's annual list of the 100 Best Companies to Work For indicates that social impact programs are increasing in popularity, because the fact of the matter is, great companies inspire their employees to give back. It's not just big companies such as Intuit, Deloitte, Patagonia, and Cisco getting into the swing of bringing their human to work by giving back. *Inc.* magazine profiled the Best Places to Work with 500 or fewer employees and discovered that even in smaller businesses, where the focus is often on making payroll and even staying afloat, 74 percent give time off for volunteering.[1]

That's a whole lot of goodwill moving through the corporate universe.

Giving back, volunteering, embracing the idea of corporate responsibility—these concepts are top of mind at companies big and small, and there is mounting evidence to support this wave as a strong business practice.

As the *New York Times* reports, "There is no room to fake it. A 2017 study on corporate social responsibility found that 65 percent of consumers check to see if a company is being authentic when it takes a stand on a social or environmental issue. That number rises to 76 percent for millennials."[2]

According to *Corporate Responsibility Magazine* (yes it exists, which by itself says a lot!), 60 percent of corporate respondents to a survey indicated that their "stakeholders expect their companies 'to engage socially in their communities,'" and more than 70 percent of those respondents also said they expect the "demand from stakeholders to increase, not decrease, in the coming years."[3]

Why wouldn't stakeholders have such expectations? A recent study by Bain & Company showed that "inspired" employees are 225 percent more productive than "engaged" ones and three times more productive than those who are "disengaged."[4] It's a beautiful thing, the way offering ourselves to others sharpens our focus and gets our wheels turning. Because we humans are such wonderfully complex creatures, there is no limit to the creative ways in which companies and teams can give back. Giving back can be as simple as donating a portion of one's proceeds or product to the needy, or it can entail multiple organizations with large coordination efforts.

With so many ways to give back, for the sake of this chapter I will highlight just three. I have, however, included a list of the top 10 ways to give back. They range from giving locally to the companies in your backyard, to giving individuals money and/ or time to donate to causes they are passionate about, to closing the office for a day to do charity work as a team. The three give-back strategies I have chosen to highlight are used by three very different companies. These businesses all share the human spirit. They knew they wanted to give back, but they wanted to get it right.

10 Ways to Give Back

There are lots of ways to give back, and they all help people feel connected to the world, their work, and themselves. Remember, regardless of your method, it's magic you are plugging into.

1. Build giving back into your company values
2. Offer your speciality to a community that needs it
3. Go local: connect with the community in your backyard
4. Do it your way: give as an individual
5. Give as a group: we're all in this together
6. Leverage technology to amplify impact
7. Involve the whole family
8. Give on location
9. Include your virtual team in the give-fest
10. Wait and see: give when so moved

Wait and See: Mack Weldon

In 2012, when the super-cool, online-centric men's underwear and clothing company Mack Weldon ("the Apple of underwear," according to the *Huffington Post*[5]) was initially launched, founder and CEO Brian Berger knew he wanted to weave giving back into his business. Still, he wasn't sure exactly how he wanted to do it. On the one hand, Berger was just starting out, so the company couldn't really afford to start giving away free stuff. Berger didn't want to just dive into an approach he didn't feel truly connected to either. So Berger and Mack Weldon waited.

From Mack Weldon's inception, being genuine and authentic was critical to Berger. "Authenticity really permeates everything that we do, from how we market, to how we price, to how we think about product innovation, to how we treat customers," Berger explained to me. He naturally wanted that same authenticity to inspire Mack Weldon's strategy for giving back. He continued, "We are all in our own ways interested in causes and being socially responsible in our private lives. How do we translate that interest into a business strategy, one that doesn't feel like we're just kind of pandering to the latest trend? How can it feel authentic?"

Berger thought about the Toms and Warby Parker BOGO models (that is, Buy One Give One), but he didn't think it made any sense for Mack Weldon, given his company's cost structure. He considered the option of donating to a men's health cause, because Mack Weldon's products are made for men. Yet that was too easy and felt a little contrived.

Therefore, instead of worrying too much about his specific method of giving back, Berger decided to focus on building a viable business, striving to ensure he and his company would have something to offer in the years to come. This appears to have been a smart strategy, since between 2013 and 2016 Mack Weldon grew 827 percent[6] and sold over one million pairs of underwear. Whenever Berger revisited the idea of social responsibility, which was often, he knew that whatever Mack Weldon eventually chose to do, he had to be able to say, "This also helps our business, our ability to build, our growth strategy, and our profitability."

Berger noticed that people like getting rid of their old underwear, socks, and T-shirts on a regular basis. Typically people throw that stuff in the garbage, because what else can they do with it? Who's going to donate used undergarments to charity or sell them on eBay? If people don't throw their old things in the garbage, they hold on to them for too long, which doesn't leave room for new items. Can you see where this is going?

In March 2017, the wait for a give-back strategy was over. Mack Weldon Recycles—"easy and effortless"—was born. Berger's authentic solution to the social impact opportunity was for Mack Weldon to partner with a third-party apparel and textile recycler called Community Recycle, a Philadelphia-based company whose objective is to keep all apparel and other soft goods out of landfills and send it to communities in need. Don't worry, the underwear itself is not recycled (that's just wrong). It's only the cotton that's recycled.

This is how it works: When customers place an order, Mack Weldon sends their wares in what they call a "two-way drawer," (*drawer*, get it?) which can be returned with up to 45 pounds of underwear or anything else from their closet at no cost to the customer. Upon receipt, Mack Weldon in turn sends the used goods off to Community Recycle to be transformed and given a new life.

In crafting his give-back strategy, Berger hypothesized that if he could help people facilitate their old-underwear clearing process, he could encourage them to buy new pairs. Next, he tested his hypothesis. The company surveyed customers of a similar age who recycled and ones who did not. Berger learned that customers who recycled added, on average, 220 percent more lifetime value to the company than those who didn't. Eureka! Berger's wait-and-see strategy was clearly worth the wait.

Berger's give-back strategy is a win-win-win. It helps customers rid their closets of old clothes, while helping them feel good about purchasing from the company. To help customers connect the dots between their actions and their social impact, every customer's profile reveals how many pounds that customer has recycled. The program has already kept 11,241 pounds of apparel out of landfills. This is equivalent to a reduction of 65,197 pounds of carbon dioxide emissions and a savings of 12.2 million gallons of water and 72 trees.[7] And, importantly, it supports Berger's goal of making Mack Weldon a profitable, growing enterprise.

Mack Weldon sells what every man needs—underwear, socks, T-shirts, and the like. They're all about basics. Their give-back strategy is pretty basic, too. Out with the old, in with the new. Everybody wins.

SPOTLIGHT

Include Your Virtual Team in the Give-Fest

Since virtual teams are becoming the norm in many industries, it's important to make everyone feel included in giving and to be mindful of creating opportunities where everyone on your team, regardless of location, can participate in giving back. VolunteerMatch is something that companies can use to match volunteer opportunities to employees anywhere in the world.

It's a business devoted to helping remote teams volunteer together.[8] While there are numerous ways for employees to give back remotely, one way VolunteerMatch facilitates this is through tree saplings: "Tree saplings are delivered to the employee's office or home, and in turn, the employee can plant the tree in their yard or local park. This gives the employee the chance to plant the tree in a special place with their family or friends on the weekend, no matter how 'remote' of a worker they are."

What a way to grow a team.

Offer Your Specialty to a Community That Needs It: General Assembly

Like many young people, Jake Schwartz, CEO of General Assembly, struggled during his twenties with the question of what he was going to do with his life. He just couldn't see how college had prepared him, and he felt lost. Eventually, channeling his personal frustrations, Schwartz created a coworking space for entrepreneurs who needed a place to both collaborate and feel connected. It wasn't long before Schwartz's space grew into something that felt more like a college campus, "a curated community where the ethos was learning by doing."

The history of General Assembly, like the history of so many successful start-ups, is an organic one. When Schwartz first opened the doors to his coworking space, he asked his fellow entrepreneurs if anyone wanted to teach a class to other start-ups. While lots of folks volunteered to teach, not many people signed up to take the classes. This makes some sense as start-ups are notoriously lean on operations, and entrepreneurs can't always take time or pay for training. But Schwartz realized that while entrepreneurs weren't lining up to take classes from their fellow in-the-know business types, people in the general public were. An idea was born.

Today, General Assembly is no longer a coworking space. It has morphed into a fast-growing training ecosystem, known as GA, which is now a leading source for training, staffing, and career transitions with campuses in 20 cities and over 35,000 graduates worldwide. In a positive twist of fate, Schwartz built something that his younger self needed. For the college grad with passion and smarts but in need of just a little more training, support, and polish—have no fear, GA is here.

Clearly, Schwartz wasn't the only one in need of a boost. The sizable market for GA-style training has helped them raise over $100 million in funding, and revenue has grown more than 40-fold since the company raised its Series A. With such success, Schwartz felt it was time to develop a distinct "social impact" arm of the company. Sure, everything GA does is for a good cause. But as a for-profit enterprise, Schwartz believed it was important to commit more explicitly to charitable giving, and with the same gusto for learning that's baked into the entire GA business.

Schwartz began reflecting on how to give back, but something felt off. He walked me through his reflection process: "There was a problem of 'who do you choose?' Do we care about women? Do we care about minorities? Do we care about inner-city, at-risk youth? Do we care about veterans? What is our cause? And I realized that I didn't want to have a cause that way. Because it just felt very myopic."

Then it hit him. Schwartz realized that, for GA, "our real asset is not the little bit of charity that we could do. The real asset is the infrastructure that we have." In other words, GA's specialty is its ability to offer large-scale training for people in need. Instead of coming up with something predictable or even something radical and new, GA simply asked itself: "How do we make training available in a different way?"

Say hello to GA's Opportunity Fund. The way it works is simple. Schwartz sets capital aside and places it into a fund that facilitates opportunities for philanthropies, corporations, and individuals to engage with GA. Entities and individuals who wish to participate pick groups they are passionate about, and GA partners with them to create a custom-tailored training program fueled by GA know-how. GA contributes its training programs at cost, and companies such as Target, Adobe, and AT&T, in turn, offer the program to their own workforce for free. It's not just Fortune 500 companies who are signing up. The iconic rapper Nas even sponsored a GA program.

This way, GA contributes its expertise to in-need audiences at cost, but GA is not tasked with choosing any particular "cause." As Schwartz explains it, this approach "aligns with the business interest. Every time there's a story about one of these great impact programs we've done, it also tells the story of what GA does at a broader level." Not only does this invite new relationships and partnerships, but as Schwartz says, "it's also something that's really cool. The stories that come out of it are just magical."

Here's just one. GA recently partnered with AT&T and Per Scholas, a nonprofit in the Bronx with a mission to "open doors to transformative technology careers for individuals from often overlooked communities." Together, GA, AT&T, and Per Scholas designed a class for people who didn't yet have the skills to take one of GA's classes. The candidates were academically unprepared for a host of reasons, but they were motivated to get into coding. CodeBridge, a free, 18-week prep course, is designed to bring students up to speed so that they can take a GA class. In the beginning, this kind of initiative was new territory for Schwartz. He wasn't familiar with the needs of this population and wasn't sure if it would work.

There is no way he could have been prepared for what came next. Not only did CodeBridge work, but it is now a thriving program. They have seen 78 students graduate from the program with more on the way. The first graduation was unlike anything Schwartz had seen or felt; he describes it as the most rewarding experience he's ever had. Period. He was incredibly moved to have been a part of something so manifestly helpful to so many people, and he wasn't the only one: "There was not a dry eye in the house."

GA brought its human to work and served as a bridge for other people to do the same.

SPOTLIGHT

Bring the Family to Work

Alston & Bird is a national law firm with an uncommon approach to giving back. First, the company "prides itself on its warm and caring atmosphere that is evident through its extensive support and flexibility for families and the community."

Alston & Bird's wide variety of benefits includes childcare, adult care or eldercare, and community service. One program that strikes me as quite powerful (and uncommon) is Family Volunteer Day, an annual event that first teaches employees and their families about a subject such as civil rights or homelessness and then follows

up the teaching with work on a mix of related
volunteer projects.

Give on Location: Faherty Goes Hands-On in Haiti

Malibu, California is a beautiful place to visit, with its sandy beaches, inviting waves for surfing, and cute boutiques and restaurants. It appeared to be the perfect place for Faherty Brand, a surf-inspired clothing company founded by twin brothers Mike and Alex Faherty, to open one of its six stores. When it was time to shoot the Faherty Brand catalog, it made sense to choose Malibu as the setting, given the company's strong connection and identification.

Before Kerry Faherty (Alex Faherty's wife) became the president of Faherty Brand, she had been a human-rights lawyer whose work took her on trips to Nigeria, Uganda, Kenya, Rwanda, Armenia, Thailand, and Haiti. As much as she loves her new role in the family business, she also misses traveling and diving into projects that make a clear difference in people's lives.

When it was time to think of a location for Faherty Brand's next catalog, Kerry Faherty remembered a friend who headed an organization in Haiti supporting communities through programs in education, healthcare, and the arts. The organization, Artists for Peace and Justice (APJ), was both inspiring and in line with what Faherty felt was missing. It occurred to her that it just might work to bring Haiti into the catalog project in some way. While she knew that Haiti is a complicated place—it's one of the poorest nations in the Western Hemisphere with a long history of political strife, not to mention the recent devastation from one of the worst earthquakes in recorded history—she wanted to share the beauty of the island, the vibrancy of the Haitian people, and the creativity of the arts community. The fact that, unbeknownst to many, Haiti has incredible beaches and great surfing cinched the deal. She would partner with APJ and shoot the catalog in Haiti.

As Faherty began planning the photo shoot in Haiti, she decided to raise $50,000 for APJ, the amount she learned would send 40 kids to school, pay a teacher's salary, and provide supplies for a year. To reach her goal, she budgeted a donation of approximately 5 percent of catalog sales for the first 90 days after the catalog's release, when business tended to boom. Though this seemed like a no-brainer to Faherty, not everyone agreed.

Faherty told me, "Some of our friends in the industry and in business expressed concern about the donation. They reminded us that we were barely profitable, so to be giving that much money back was kind of crazy." But Faherty trusted herself, knowing that her customers would love the idea. She was determined.

On March 6, 2017, Faherty Brand brought 10 team members and friends to Haiti. They visited multiple locations on the island, both for the shoot itself and to surf with local kids. The team came back truly "inspired, [and] humbled." Later, when I asked Faherty to characterize the power of making such a trip, one which even included a dicey moment or two, she continued, "Running a business is really hard, and it's easy to get isolated and inundated by your own day-to-day stresses. You kind of forget what is happening in other parts of the world, and what other struggles people have to go through on a day-to-day basis."

In the end, $50,000 was delivered to APJ. A local Haitian school has named one of its classrooms the Faherty Room. "Raising the money is something that we're really proud of as a brand," says Faherty. This give-back effort proved to be a project every team member at Faherty Brand rallied around, and Faherty herself looks forward to returning to Haiti with her team at some point. After all, this trip built strong new relationships, both within and outside of the company.

Giving back is part of being human. Think of finding your own company's approach as just another opportunity to discover who you are and what you stand for. Take the time to do it authentically and in line with what you believe is good for people and great for business, and it just might change the world.

SPOTLIGHT

Drive to Give Back

Subaru, the global car manufacturer, is a brand associated with outdoorsy, family life. Its tagline is "Love. It's what makes a Subaru a Subaru." Can't get much more down-home than that! It makes sense that Subaru would commit to finding ways to amplify this feel-good message.

As reported in the *New York Times*, Subaru had 512 employees volunteer for 105 events at 46 different organizations between January and September of 2017. One of these events was in Camden, New Jersey, a poor city a few minutes from Subaru's headquarters in Cherry Hill.

"Seventy-four employees donated 500 hours to build three Habitat for Humanity homes."[9]

Subaru takes its employees' passions very seriously. Instead of just noting hours volunteered, Subaru enlisted the help of a software platform called Blackbaud. Blackbaud helps them covert their raw data into actual impact. They aren't satisfied with just making their employees feel good. They want to drive actual change for real people and to see the love. It's what makes them who they are.

HUMAN ACTION PLAN

1. **Discover.** The best give-back strategies are discovered, not designed. What I mean by that is that such programs are most resonant when they are intrinsically tied to the mission of the business, as with the companies highlighted in this chapter. And this connection may well not appear in the early days of the company. So be patient, keep your ears, eyes, and mind open, and discover a strategy that adds value and depth to what you already do.

2. **Involve.** Bringing your employees in on the ground floor of the discovery and design of your give-back strategy is a great way to get them engaged. Jessica Mah, CEO of InDinero (a software company that provides back-office solutions to small businesses), has a rotating culture board where employees weigh in on a variety of cultural issues including how to give back. Business Talent Group, a global consulting marketplace that employs many millennials, empowered their employees to design a program. If you want employees to care, get them involved.

3. **Share and listen.** Don't forget to tell the world (especially your employees and customers) about how you're giving back. Share your company's impact with employees and clients at meetings and on your website. Share stories about all the great

ways your company and its employees are giving back to the world as part of your recruitment efforts.

Also be sure to listen for ordinary stories around the office of how giving back has affected your employees, whether or not they are part of company-sponsored initiatives. Then tell those stories as well. Shine a light on employees who have gone above and beyond, and share the impact that your organization is having on the world.

Sharing stories about individual employee impact and companywide efforts encourages your team to give back even more, amplifying the amount of good your organization can do for the world.

7

Disconnect to Reconnect: Where There's a Will, There's a Way

Human beings need a break. They need time for their minds to wander aimlessly, to enjoy one another's company, to sleep in, or to do nothing. In her 2017 book *Bored and Brilliant*, Manoush Zomorodi writes that "we get our most original ideas when we stop the constant stimulation, and let ourselves get bored."[1] Neuroscientists have confirmed this, showing that allowing our brains to take a break from the constant stimulation of productivity benefits us in many ways.[2]

For instance, in observing 35 executives, entrepreneurs, and influencers who went device free for a week, researchers realized that "people tended to make significant changes to their lives when they were offline for a while. Some decided to make big changes in their career or relationships, while others decided to recommit to health and fitness." Not only did people make big life changes, but researchers also saw small adjustments, such as better posture, more eye contact, and increased energy, after as few as three days. People retrained their bodies to connect face to face with the humans around them. Maybe those small adjustments weren't so small after all.[3]

An article from the *New York Times* points out that constant engagement with technology actually diminishes our brain's ability to process memory and learning. "When people keep their brains busy with digital input, they are forfeiting downtime that could allow them to better learn and remember information, or come up with new ideas."[4]

Interestingly some cutting-edge coffee shops, the home to so many "productive" digital nomads, are taking the radical step of turning off their Wi-Fi so their customers will talk to one another. Jimson Bienenstock, the president of HotBlack, a Toronto coffee shop, explained to the *New York Times*: "It's about creating a social vibe. . . . We're a vehicle for human interaction, otherwise [we're] just a commodity."[5]

A so-called "social vibe" is what we humans need. Right? But how we resist!

A recent survey from the employer-reviewing site Glassdoor identified that the average U.S. employee who receives vacation and paid time off (i.e., 91 percent of full-time employees[6]) has taken only about half of his or her eligible vacation in the past 12 months.[7] In 2017, the research and advocacy coalition Project Time Off found that "the 55 percent of under-vacationed Americans left a total 658 million vacation days unused. It is the biggest number Project Time Off has ever reported."[8] Word to the wise—Project Time Off also learned that employees who took vacations were 6.5 percent more likely to get a promotion.

If you happen to be in a management position, your practice of disconnection has an even bigger effect. A 2014 *Harvard*

Business Review study of 19,000 people discovered that the mere 25 percent of managers who modeled sustainable work practices were the ones whose direct reports were happier, healthier, and more engaged at work.[9]

Any way you slice it, intentional disconnection is good for business.

Why do more and more companies have to nudge and even badger their employees to turn off their phones and take vacations? Are we just so incredibly passionate about our work and deeply fulfilled that we can't bear to tear ourselves away? Not exactly.

While it's true that some people and some industries just skew toward high-octane work habits, we all wrestle with a certain problem, something that won't come as a surprise to anyone reading this book. You guessed it. Project Time Off reports that "as internet adoption goes up, vacation usage goes down." The report continues, "America's culture of busyness has been driven in large part by connectivity, so much so that the Pew Research Center determined nearly half of office-based workers say that email has increased the amount of time they spend working."[10]

Our technology, as incredible as it is, is keeping an already workaholic culture more tethered to our roving desks than ever. Now, whether we're in the office, on the train, walking down the street, at the table with our kids, or even in bed with our partner, we receive work calls, emails, and texts. All too often, we answer. We seek the next dopamine hit that comes from GSD (Getting Stuff Done) instead of, well, . . . other pleasures. A 2016 survey by the app developer Delvv found that almost a third of Americans "would rather give up sex for three months than give up their smartphone for one week."[11]

As I always say, left to our own "devices" (excuse the pun), we just aren't connecting. We also aren't disconnecting. Smart companies understand that it's bad for the bottom line to have people working 24/7, because overwork leads to burnout, lack of engagement, and attrition. Still, in a culture where we check our phones an average of 47 times per day,[12] even a little disconnection is a lot to ask for.

Here's the good news: where there's a will, there's a way.

Start as You Mean to Go On: Walking the Walk(er)

When my kids were little, I read a book by the British pediatrician Penelope Leach, who made this excellent recommendation: "Start as you mean to go on." That is to say, start off on the right foot. For example, if it's important to you that your kids have impeccable table manners as teens, then as soon as they first sit in their high chair, begin the training—*Cheerios stay on the tray, please.* Otherwise, when you think it's the right time to begin teaching manners, it might be a bit too late, and you will have to waste precious time undoing bad habits. I learned that a clean slate is often the very best kind of slate for teaching and imprinting values.

The same mindset goes for businesses. Whether you are launching a company or entering a new phase in your business or perhaps simply tackling a new project, a key to success is "starting as you mean to go on." This, of course, implies that you know how you want to go on. The importance of knowing who you are as a business—knowing what your values are—cannot be overstated.

Tristan Walker, CEO of Walker & Company, a health and beauty brand that Walker refers to as the "Procter & Gamble of people of color," is one of the most sought-after speakers on the business stage today—for good reason. Walker himself has a great backstory, and he is also as sharp as a tack. His business has raised over $33 million in outside investment,[13] and 2017 revenue grew over 200 percent from the prior year.[14] Evidently, Walker has always known what he wanted. And he started as he meant to go on.

The son of a single mother who struggled to make ends meet, Walker had the intellect and passion to land a full ride to Hotchkiss, a prestigious prep school in Lakeville, Connecticut. After college at SUNY Stony Brook, he attended the Stanford Graduate School of Business. At the tender age of 32, he founded the very cool and successful start-up he now leads. And as if that weren't enough, he also strives to lead a fulfilling personal life.

How does he do it? First, Walker doesn't buy the notion that start-up culture needs to be a burnout, work-'til-you-drop culture. In fact, quite the opposite. Walker, a founder after my own heart, established his company's core values right out of the gate, one of which is wellness, a subject to which I've already devoted some ink (Chapter Five). He defines it as, "we eat well, we sleep well, we keep fit, and we care to help and support each other and our families." In keeping with this value, Walker swears he leaves work by 6 p.m. most days.

In a world where most people pride themselves or even define themselves by sacrificing the proverbial "everything" for their start-up, how did Walker do this? His very matter-of-fact answer: "We started the company . . . when my wife was pregnant. I started by reflecting on the things that mattered to me." In other words, in looking ahead, he checked in with himself. "First and foremost, there are three things that are important to me," he explained, "my faith, my family, my work—in that order. I don't do anything else." Walker made a very human commitment to himself, early on.

When I asked him how he institutionalized such healthy values, he said, "It's easy." Walker shared, "I never had a father that really raised me. So I was like, I'm not going to let anything get in the way of that, because this is the order of things that are important to me, and I made that clear to everybody. It comes from the top."

He knew how he wanted his company culture to feel and function, and he started as he meant to go on.

With such a clear internal compass, Walker makes disconnecting while running a business look easy. The importance of wellness was put to the test when Walker opted for a three-month paternity leave right at the beginning of his tenure as CEO. Ultimately he wanted other new parents to do the same, and he knew that if he didn't lead by example, it would be difficult if not impossible to get others to disconnect and take the time. After his leave, Walker found it funny and ironic to return to a company that was, as he put it, "operat[ing] better without me . . . ! When I took that paternity leave I knew that I had to set that precedent. I was the first one to do that at the company, mother or father."[15]

Moreover, once Walker was back in his seat at work, he continued to "walk the walk" of disconnection. Each night, he arrives home in time for dinner, choosing to ignore email in the evening unless he is working on something time sensitive. He encourages all his employees to do the same.

Walker recognizes that running a company, whether in start-up mode or otherwise, has some unpredictability baked in. "It's not always nirvana," he admitted. At Walker & Company, on occasion everyone is expected to stay a little later and pitch in. By walking the walk though, Walker communicates a certain wisdom. He knows that his success depends on creating and maintaining a genuine culture of human dis/connection. In

Walker's words, "If you're not taking care of yourself or your family, you're not taking care of business."

Now that's honoring relationships.

Design for Disconnection:
Rowland + Broughton, Architects

John Rowland and Sarah Broughton are the married cofounders of Rowland+Broughton (R+B), a highly successful, award-winning residential and commercial architecture firm based in Colorado.

Rowland and Broughton have been the devoted, hard-working principals of their firm since they established it 15 years ago. They were accustomed to working over 60 hours a week and to going out nightly to socialize with existing clients or develop new business. They have long been happy to run themselves ragged for the good of their business, answering emails all weekend. As Broughton put it, "This is a design company, yes, but it is also a client services business," and developing relationships and staying connected to clients is key. Rowland and Broughton were on top of their game, and life was good. Until it wasn't.

Five years ago, the dynamic duo felt a shift occurring at their firm. While experts believe that 10 percent turnover is considered about right for a firm such as R+B,[16] attrition had risen to around 30 percent, and this was hurting the mental and financial health of the firm. R+B hired a consultant to figure out what was happening. They were told, "You've established a great design firm, but you've got to really start working on your culture."

They soon discovered that one of the main contributors to the attrition was that employees felt they always had to be "on." The way their productivity was measured, typical of most professional services firms, was via hours billable to clients. Therefore, any ancillary responsibilities and growth initiatives, workplace committees, conferences, and the like went unreported and essentially unappreciated. Given the many hours the devoted employees committed, they all felt burned out. And they left.

Something had to change.

Rowland and Broughton took the feedback to heart. While it would cost time and money, they were ready to invest heavily to save their firm. As a first step, they hired a head of culture, something unheard of in their industry. This worked. Soon a culture of fun, inspiration, thoughtful performance reviews, and even sabbaticals had been woven into the fabric of the firm. Disconnecting for greater connection was working.

Next, Rowland and Broughton set out to develop, implement, and ensure a *system* of maintaining balance (one of their values, by the way). They used software to track all employee activities to ensure that *all* the work expended was appreciated, not merely billable client hours. With this system, if people get out of balance, perhaps by working way over their allotted 40-some hours, they might even get pinged and told to disconnect.

Major progress!

As the principals were basking proudly in their new culture and their employees' newfound, healthy balance at work, it didn't occur to them that they themselves needed to change. The two were understandably quite surprised when the executive team, including the directors of culture, of finance, and of operations, approached them and declared, "Now we need to target the 12 people who are still . . . working way too much. Which includes the two of you."

The problem was so close to home that it was a little tricky to grasp. While pointing to all the ways everyone around them should change, they failed to see how their "committed" work habits were creating stress for their employees. They were so busy getting everyone else's life in balance that they picked up all the slack and neglected themselves. They realized a very important lesson, one that every leader and CEO should take to heart: those charged with setting the tone of an organization are more than just hard-working members of a team. As leaders, what they do matters. Exponentially.

These days, Rowland and Broughton remain conscious of the challenges of ensuring a human workplace, and they strive to regularly respect their goal of a 40-hour workweek. The firm has grown to about 40 people across multiple offices in Colorado, and they can now point to their first employee with 10 years of tenure. To evolve, they are considering the launch of a four-week paid sabbatical program for long-term employees. To see how this type of program would work, not just in theory but in reality, Rowland and Broughton decided to take a sabbatical themselves.

After months of planning and getting their ducks in a row, in September 2017 Rowland and Broughton traveled to Europe for a month, disconnecting to connect to art and culture, letting their minds wander, and getting their creative juices flowing. I spoke to Broughton a few weeks after her return, and she was still on cloud nine. Her brain was spinning with new ideas, and she feverishly described a new project she was working on, one that brought inspiration from the Greek island of Mykonos to the mountains of Colorado. Broughton revealed to me that one of the best parts of the sabbatical was that they each had time to think. They were able to reflect upon what they wanted for themselves as people and to think about the future of the firm. This disconnected time is so important and, sadly, uncommon.

Broughton explained another benefit of the sabbatical. While the two were away, their emails went to their assistants and were then redirected to other team members. Broughton saw only the most important, time-sensitive, mission-critical emails. When she returned to the office, she wondered, *Why does this have to change?* Then she realized, *It doesn't!* Rowland and Broughton are now only copied on certain types of emails, though they are always available for their employees and clients if there's a problem. Their employees benefit from this policy too, as they are encouraged to develop the necessary skills to step into new roles.

The happy couple returned from their sabbatical rested, inspired, and eager to dive back in. This set the tone for the firm, modeling a mindset for a place where disconnection is supported.

R+B has now progressed from being regarded as a top design firm to being regarded as a top design firm with a strong culture, which as we have seen, is good for the bottom line. Today at R+B, revenues are up, attrition is down, and over 60 percent of the firm's work is repeat business.

A business like that is putting relationships to work. Remember that the very fundamental element of this book that we keep coming back to is *relationships*. Your relationship to yourself, and your relationship to your employees. If you're not leading by example and showing your employees that it's okay to disconnect, to live your life outside of work, they won't know that they can do the same.

Tweaks and Techniques from Companies Working Hard to Disconnect

There are many different ways for employees to disconnect from work. Ideally, a company will start as it means to go on. However, if a company needs to fix an existing culture of overload, that's okay, too. The first step is to incorporate disconnection into the company values. Next, be sure everyone does it—staff, managers, and executives. Finally, don't disconnect on the sly. Celebrate the joys that come from disconnecting!

Encourage Employees to Go Home Without Supper

While many Silicon Valley companies boast about their many and varied on-site restaurants or dining options, Slack, the fast-growing messaging connection platform, has taken a different approach. The motto that hangs on a sign in Slack's San Francisco headquarters reads: *Work hard and go home.*

The idea is that if you don't serve dinner, it's more likely your employees will leave the office to have dinner with family and friends. When I visited Slack, I spoke with a new employee who had just become a first-time dad. He, in particular, spoke excitedly about this disconnect philosophy, noting how very different it was from his other experiences in Silicon Valley. Burnout is real, and encouraging employees to disconnect is good for business.

Make Employees Cry (Happy Tears, of Course) by Closing the Office

In 2015, REI, the outdoor retailer, made big news in the retail community when it decided to close its stores on the biggest shopping day of the year, Black Friday. REI announced it wanted its employees to #optoutside and be with family and friends. One of REI's store managers in Bloomington, Minnesota, Brian Harrower, said this was the first time in his 25-year retail career that he was able to be with friends and family on the Friday after Thanksgiving.[17]

Similarly, Food52, the digital food and lifestyle brand I wrote about earlier, closes up shop for one week twice a year, sending all of its staff packing. To encourage and promote disconnection, they even have a couple of hashtags (#F52winterweek and #F52summerweek) to celebrate vacations and their culture of disconnection.

No More Email Pile-Up

People are often reluctant to take vacation time, sometimes for even as few as 24 hours, because they don't want to come back to the nightmare of an inbox overflowing with emails. Respecting this legitimate worry, companies like Huffington Post and Daimler use a tool that automatically deletes emails received during a vacation. The software sends a message directing people to resend their messages, after the employee's vacation.

This bold move honors relationships and the need to disconnect. Employees don't feel obliged to run around looking for a signal on the beach in a fruitless effort to preempt email pile-up. They just don't have any!

Send Friendly Reminders

In conversation with one of Google's product managers, I learned that when he hits 20 days of unused vacation, he receives a reminder from the human resources department instructing him to take some time off. Seriously. He continues to receive a "nudge" every 10 days or so until he actually takes a vacation.

What's he waiting for?

Leave Loudly

To reduce "presenteeism" (yes, it's a thing), junior employees need to see their leaders go home. Robbert Rietbroek, CEO of PepsiCo Australia and New Zealand, implemented "Leaders

Leaving Loudly" to ensure leaders felt comfortable going home and to get them to announce it to their teams. "For instance, if I occasionally go at 4 p.m. to pick up my daughters, I will make sure I tell the people around me, 'I'm going to pick up my children.' Because if it's okay for the boss, then it's okay for middle management and new hires."[18]

Disconnecting and embracing values that support it are something to celebrate.

Don't Leave a Vacation Day on the Table

Barri Rafferty, CEO of Ketchum Inc, the global public relations firm, believes one should never leave a vacation day on the table. Her motto was put to the test on the first day she became the CEO in January 2018, as her new gig coincided with a long-scheduled "bucket list" trip to Tanzania. While some may view this as bad timing, worthy of rescheduling, Rafferty saw it as an opportunity to send a message (loud and clear) about the importance of disconnecting. In her very first memo to employees as the CEO, she wrote, "I believe in taking vacations. . . . You'll be better off and our clients will benefit because of it." Talk about starting as you mean to go on! She also explained that "people need downtime to let their brains think differently—especially in creative industries."

For Rafferty, traveling is what gives her that creative inspiration: "Being in different places, with different food, art, and culture."

And if All Else Fails . . . Maybe Even Pay to Play

FullContact, a Denver-based contact management platform, pays its employees $7,500 to take time off. But there's a catch with this neat little payment: no email on the beach. Employees must truly disconnect.[19]

In similar fashion, Manhattan-based SteelHouse Advertising, pioneer of a cloud-based advertising platform, pays employees $2,000 to take their vacation days. CEO Mark Douglas says, "It's one thing to say 'You have three weeks vacation,' like most companies do. . . . It's another thing to say 'You have cash, and if you don't go on vacation and spend this money, the money literally goes to waste.' It's another level of saying this is real." Not surprisingly, this human policy of encouraging disconnection is good for business. "We have virtually zero turnover," says Douglas."[20]

🤝 HUMAN ACTION PLAN

1. **Lead by example.** If you are a leader, leave on time, take that vacation, take an email hiatus over the weekend, and make a "big deal" out of it. Whether you "leave loudly," send out a company-wide email, or share vacation photos on social media like the execs at Food52, be sure to brag loudly and proudly about your ability to disconnect. Your employees are taking cues from their leaders, and if you don't disconnect, no one will.

2. **Deal with it.** One of the biggest obstacles to employees unplugging is the nightmare that they are faced with when they log back on. So just telling people to take the weekend off won't work unless there is a plan in place to deal with the digital pile-up. Like Huffington Post and Daimler, you can delete vacation emails, or assign someone else to respond to them. Does it make sense for employees to check in once a day? Or is it better to completely disconnect? One tip that I have personally used is to set up a new email account during my vacation that only my assistant and family members have, so when I check it I won't be sidetracked with emails that can wait until I return.

3. **Keep track.** If you can't measure it, you can't manage it. Giving employees unlimited vacation might seem like a way to encourage disconnection,

but sometimes it has the opposite effect. Set up a system to track when employees are taking vacation, and have conversations with those who are not, and find out why. Instead of compensating employees for unused vacation days, consider offering them an incentive to take it, see what happens, and share the stories. Some employees may not realize it's been 12 months since their last day off!

8

Space Matters: Curating Connection Starts with the Water Cooler

We shape our buildings; thereafter they shape us.
—WINSTON CHURCHILL

There is much ado about office space these days. Should yours be "open" or traditional? Should you include standing desks or good, old-fashioned cubicles? How much time do your teams need for collaboration, and how much for concentrated work, and what are the implications for the design of your conference rooms? The answers vary, depending on who you ask. I recommend making your workplace more human by designing for interaction. After all, that's why we're all in the same building, isn't it? I feel so strongly about this point that I would say that if you aren't going to use your space well, there's barely a reason to have it in the first place. You may as well just give everyone a laptop and a Starbucks card.

It's pretty simple: if you want to get the most out of the people in your company, pay attention to space. A survey by Steelcase discovered that only 11 percent of workers surveyed were highly satisfied with their work environment.[1] And we know what happens when workers are unsatisfied! On the other hand, an office environment that fosters connection can raise employee productivity by at least 25 percent.[2]

Since the human company curates connection, that is how we should consider our space. If you have the good fortune of starting a building project from scratch, you can channel your inner Steve Jobs, strategically placing bathrooms to encourage "serendipitous personal encounters." If your office is already fully operational, consider tweaking it for interaction—a kitchen here, a water cooler there. Design your space to help people establish the friendships that benefit us and our companies in countless ways, ranging from lower attrition to higher engagement and job satisfaction.[3]

Read on to get some tips from companies who have done just that.

Line It Up: Aligning Space with Mission and Values

Because we are so affected by our environment, our space is a very personal terrain. While every business needs to pay attention to how its employees interact with the world around them, some of us are more tuned in to the subtleties. These are the people we can learn from.

When Anthony Casalena, CEO of Squarespace, was a college student at the University of Maryland, he wanted to build a website that both looked great and worked well. First, he did what the rest of us do—he looked to existing web platforms to find one he liked. However, being a gifted programmer with an eye for design (a winning combination), he couldn't find one to his liking. So he built his own.

Fast-forward 15 years and millions of users later, and Casalena's company Squarespace is a winner. The company employs over 550 people[4] and has been recognized as one of Wealthfront's Career-Launching Companies for 2018,[5] Hired's #1 New York–based brand in 2017,[6] and one of Fortune's 100 Best Workplaces for Millennials in 2015.[7] Given the growth, at one point employees became spread out across six floors in four different buildings. However, "Squarespace prides itself on being a collaborative work environment," says Casalena, and the spread-out nature of the office environment was not working. As he explains, "When you are split across six floors, and it takes 15 minutes to get to a meeting, it changes who you talk with and how you talk to them."[8]

In order to tame the chaos of this approaching sprawl, and to ensure that Squarespace could maintain its culture as it continued to scale, Casalena enlisted the architects at A+I, a design firm in New York City. The result is now one of the most talked-about workspaces in the city, a sophisticated, black-and-white (with a few splashes of green), very grown-up space spanning three floors. The space is a testament to the Squarespace tagline: Make it beautiful.[9]

Whenever A+I tackles a new project, its people spend months getting to know a company's values and mission. This mindset made Squarespace a perfect client. Brad Zizmor, one of A+I's cofounders, told me they worked very hard to ensure a "very strong connection between the values that Caselena brings to his brand . . . and what is being expressed in the architecture."

A+I calls this "walking the mission statement." Casalena was on board. As he recalls, "I wanted to design a space that reflected Squarespace's identity as a brand."

This sort of intentional values-to-space mapping is surely much easier when you have the expert assistance of a design firm such as A+I, but the concept is something every business can apply. As a writer for *The Business Journals*, a leading business publication for millennials, explains, "If your company is committed to a cleaner environment, your workspace should punctuate that by emphasizing sustainability and conservation. If your firm is in the healthcare industry, your workspace should emphasize natural light, standing desk options, and encourage physical movement in general."[10]

When Casalena approached A+I he made it clear that he wanted the space to reflect his belief that "design is not a luxury," which also happens to be their #1 corporate value. Casalena also wanted the new space to "line up" with his company by reflecting the way his employees worked—equal parts wild collaboration and intense solitude—a working style Zizmor referred to as a "binary state of being." The folks at Squarespace needed to be able to turn these two different states of being on and off, and their space needed to be attuned to this need. After months of discussion and returning time and time again to the literal drawing board, they hatched a plan, the likes of which A+I had never envisioned before. In most workplaces, the rooms where people do their solitary work (i.e., their offices) line the exterior walls, and the interior space is used for common areas, walkways, etc. At Squarespace, nobody has a private office now, not even Casalena. However, people still need to do quiet work, so the entire exterior wall of the three-floored space is wide open, bright, and quiet, available for everyone to use as they wish. All the common spaces—the conversation pods, conference rooms, etc.—are nestled into the interior space. As employees move closer to the exterior and closer to the light, the office provides more private space for working in quiet mode. Zizmor mentioned to me as we toured the space, "We've never done a project where there are no rooms that exist against the windows."

A design decision like switching offices for common space might not sound like much, but the experience is powerful and speaks very clearly to a culture of transparency, community, and intentionality. This is evidently a place that both values the power of solo concentration while still honoring relationships.

In addition, A+I "lined up" the flow and set-up of the main areas with Squarespace's values, from the black and white of the bathrooms to the glass-walled boardroom. Every single detail of Squarespace's offices is connected to the overall vision of the brand. Just as Squarespace's web products favor simplicity and the power of editing, so too does the space. You'll find no clutter, and no cabinets to hide the clutter. Whiteboards are integrated into walls. Each and every aspect of the space is functional and beautiful.

Even as understatement and simplicity reign, the office was designed to be aligned with the brand. The space says "Squarespace" in the design itself, so nothing in the office needs to explicitly do so. When I visited the office, Casalena pointed out, "You'll notice there are very few branded elements in our office."

For a company where good design *is* the brand, space really matters. The values, the mission, and the space are all lined up. It's a kind of simple elegance that makes Squarespace products what they are. After all, that's what Squarespace stands for.

SPOTLIGHT

Life Imitates Art

Max Berger is the senior founding partner at Bernstein Litowitz Berger & Grossmann, LLP (BLB&G), a law firm dedicated to prosecuting securities fraud. When it was time to design BLB&G's new office space, Berger wanted to create a legacy and a place where "young people would want to come to work." He envisioned a space reflective of their values, their sense of themselves as a firm that works hard to protect people.

The reception area of BLB&G's new office now prominently features a large painting of Batman by Nicole Charbonnet, a New Orleans artist. Berger shared with me, "We think of ourselves as protecting Gotham, as protecting people who are victims of economic crimes. When I saw this new space, I saw the reception area, and I knew that is where Batman would go."

Holy human, Batman!

Mix It Up: Intentional Chaos for Human Connection

Some things never change. Whether we're middle schoolers in the lunchroom or grown men and women with big jobs at fancy firms, it's the rare human being who doesn't have an opinion about where they sit. Workplaces today offer a variety of options to these opinionated workers—assigned seats, unassigned seats, perhaps even roving seats. Small rooms, big rooms. Offices may offer "office hoteling" (also called hot-desking or free-addressing), providing desks and other workspaces on an as-needed basis, booked either through a reservation system or on a first-come, first-served basis. And some offices offer the "no seats" model, where nobody comes to work, per se, but employees are directed to one of the many coworking spaces cropping up in the sharing/gig economy.

As with everything else in the human workplace, when it comes to a company's choice of seating arrangement, the one designed with intention and purpose typically wins. Willy-nilly seating is a far cry from intentional chaos when it comes to human connection.

Investopedia's ROI on the Seating Chart

David Siegel is the CEO of Investopedia, the exhaustive online guide to smart investing, and he is a fan of a purposeful mix-it-up strategy when it comes to space design. Investopedia's 80 New York employees sit in an open-office design. Siegel takes mixing it up to the max by encouraging people to sit in places that arguably go against the grain of how companies are usually organized. He believes this is important because work is becoming so much more complex and less siloed, which means that people need to interact and collaborate with a broader range of people and departments. To him, it's a leader's job to think beyond an employee's job description and reporting structure when placing them in a seating chart. Siegel explained in a chat with me, "People build relationships with those with the most similar backgrounds, careers, and interests. As a leader, you need to break this paradigm."

Siegel's purposeful, uncommon take on work translates into seating people near those he wants them to collaborate with, not necessarily near those an employee reports to. For instance, Siegel explained to me that at Investopedia "our social media team reports into marketing, but sits with editorial. Our product team reports into our SVP, Product, but the team sits with the business it supports. The more people sit outside of their reporting functions, [the more] the barriers between those functions [aka those *people*] will melt away. And that is good for business."

While Siegel has strong opinions on "mixing it up" to create strong organizational connections, he also believes that employees should have a voice in who sits around them, as neighbors can have a significant impact on productivity. (Think, for example, of the experience of sitting in the quiet car of an Amtrak train . . . next to someone talking on the phone). Because staff has tripled over the last two years, Investopedia has moved into a number of new offices. Every time the company moves to a new building (or whenever a major group gets moved), Siegel sends his employees a three-question survey about preferences and habits, just to ensure that people and their office neighbors are a good match for each other.

Since, as Siegel says, "employees are in the office eight, nine hours a day . . . good neighbors make for better morale." Even though he runs a mix-it-up kind of office, Siegel advises, "Don't let your office seating chart be like a game of musical chairs." He and his office manager fastidiously review and consider the best place for every single new employee to sit.

The effort and investment is worth it to Siegel. He knows that space matters.

SPOTLIGHT

Design for Belonging

Airbnb uses space as a way to communicate their commitment to travel and the mission of belonging. Meeting rooms are inspired by actual listings from around the world (e.g., a chateau in France or a café in Mumbai), and employees play a key role in choosing which listings to bring to life. In some cases, employees are given a budget and a liason from the facilities team to help design, select materials for, and build the meeting rooms. Talk about a hands-on role! Mark Levy, the former head of employee experience at Airbnb, shared with me that "when your meeting room feels like somebody's living room or dining room, you feel like you are creating a space for belonging rather than just a place for a meeting." So true!

Levy emphasized that space is "just one more way we have brought our mission and business into the workplace and how we have engaged our employees."

DoSomething Reaps the Benefits of Mixing It Up

DoSomething.org, a nonprofit connecting millennials and Gen Z with volunteer opportunities, has an open floor plan and assigned desks, and their 60 employees are encouraged to mix it up. Actually, they are more than encouraged. Every six months a formal swapping of desks occurs. They've termed this exchange "the Reaping," named tongue in cheek after a community-wide reckoning from the hit series The Hunger Games.

At 9:30 a.m. on the day of the Reaping, names are drawn one by one, and whenever an employee's name is pulled, he or she has 15 seconds to find a new seat. The DoSomething contributors to *The XYZ Factor*, a book highlighting insights into their corporate world, explain that "it's a day of nerves and excitement. People come to work very early on the day of the Reaping. They consider the options, strategize, and hope they get picked early! It's a great opportunity to press restart—kind of like spring cleaning. Staff members clear out papers and clutter, polish old desks, and arrive at a sparkling clean new desk by 10 a.m. A clear, spacious desk gives us a clear, spacious brain."

Desk swapping happens formally, office-wide, but pressing restart conceptually is also part of the DoSomething culture. Whenever an employee feels stuck, he or she is encouraged to pick up and move to various places around the office. It offers a sense of freedom, a path to explore different seating options, including standing desks and soft couches. *The XYZ Factor* contributors note that "employees are like liquid, flowing through the office all day long. They are encouraged to develop work habits in spaces that suit them, and employees who are connected to a space where they do their best work want to come to work every day."

Mixing It Up Is Better at Betterment

At Betterment, the online, automated investing service, CEO Jon Stein agrees with the idea of mixing it up. Many of the programs and policies at Betterment are designed to increase cross-functional knowledge. The intentional design includes where people sit: employees sit in "pods," which are general areas or groupings, and assignments shift every four to six months. The Betterment handbook states that "a simple thing like a change in work environment can frequently lead to a bigger change in perspective." Betterment wants its employees to know that "a change in perspective also helps foster transparency, camaraderie, and respect between our different departments. When the senior product designer sits next to the marketing manager, across from the newest software engineer, everyone develops a better understanding of the important role that we each play every day."

In addition to mixing it up in the office through thoughtful space design, Betterment also engages employees who need to get away and take a breather. Betterment has an account at Breather, an app that people can use to rent office space by the day or by the hour. This gives teams the option of booking an off-site office through the app whenever employees really need a change of scenery to do a deep dive on an important project or to take their team off-site.

This is uncommon flexibility, and it works for Betterment. Now, mixing it up sounds good, but if you don't like the pressure of the Reaping and don't have the time to redesign your seating plan every few months, technology might be able to help.

Big Data = Better Seating

Ben Waber is the CEO of Humanyze, a company that helps businesses use data to make better decisions. Waber is certain that the future of work will involve artificial intelligence. What will that look like? In Waber's estimation, it will look like the current flexible-seating office that many tech companies already use, except instead of employees deciding where they will sit on any given day, there would be an AI-generated suggestion based on what is considered most productive and efficient.

Waber says, "If you go there, the right stuff is probably going to happen. You'll probably bump into the right people. You'll probably be near people you need to work with that day. Not that any algorithm is going to be 100 percent predictive, but with those little nudges we can actually be significantly more productive and effective in our work."[11]

I don't know when or if we will ever achieve a broad adoption of technology-driven seating plans. But I do know that dynamic, mixed-up, connection-induced seating inspires humans in the workplace.

Don't Mess It Up: Create Rules of the Road

Once you've designed the perfect space aligned to your company values and figured out where everyone should sit, you're done, right? Wrong! Unfortunately, mastering this space business is not as easy as "if you build it they will connect." It is true that the space itself matters (a lot), but you won't get the results you seek if you don't consider the implementation, roll-out, and communications. In other words, don't forget the human part.

I remember my experience a few years ago visiting one of the Silicon Valley tech companies that offered an array of options for its employees, who could select a different building each day for cuisine from different parts of the world—sushi one day, Indian the next, and Mexican the day after that. And yet the employees I spoke to ate lunch in the *same* cafeteria pretty much every day—the one that was the closest to where they sat. While I'm sure the designers of the space thought they were inspiring collaboration by inviting people to make the trek across campus, it's a shame many of us humans can be so set in our ways.

Creating and communicating rules of the road around how to use the space we've carefully designed gives companies the best shot at getting a real return on their investment.

Protocols can help them "not mess it up."

SPOTLIGHT

Highlight It in the Handbook

Food52, the online platform curating and creating community around food, has an amazing office designed like a home. It features not one, but two kitchens. And just like in a home, Food52 enforces rules of the road like those we all grew up with such as "no dishes in the sink." Food52 includes a section in their handbook on how the various office spaces should be used. The Open Lounge, for example, is used for "working, casual meetings, company gatherings, and oh, for secret naps." The handbook presents photos of each space. Providing these rules of the road increases the company's ability to curate connection.

Rolling Out Workspace360

With over 70,000 employees globally, CBRE is one of the world's largest commercial real estate services and investment firms. CBRE should know a thing or two about what it takes to make a space work well, and they do. Workplace360 is the name of a new program being implemented in CBRE's offices. This program has moved CBRE away from a traditional office setup featuring "large private offices lin[ing] the windows with administrative support cubicles in the center"[12] to a high-tech, free-address system where no one has a desk or even file cabinets. This presented a huge challenge for many CBRE employees, who were accustomed to decorating their offices with family photos and work-related awards symbolic of years of hard work. Previously, everyone had a human place to hang their human hat, but their old-school office plan came at a price—it was only occupied 51 percent of the time.[13]

CBRE leadership set out to see how it could make a change for the better. The first office to implement Workplace360 was CBRE headquarters in Los Angeles. Lew Horne, the president of CBRE, Southern California, was tasked with leading the charge. Horne was smart enough to recognize that a key to success was not just "what" was being done, but "how" the change was implemented. Horne understood how hard the transition would be for many of the long-term employees (including himself), those who had always had an office with file drawers, and especially for those who weren't super tech-savvy. He also knew that for many of the firm's rising stars, the aspiration for that big corner office was one of the carrots that kept them plowing forward. Horne's conclusion was simple: "We've got to change. Let's figure it out together."[14]

Therefore, Horne made a significant investment in the "how." That's just another way of saying he engaged the human element of the change. He knew that people's potential resistance to change could derail the whole program, and he respected what could make them resistant.

Step one was to engage the skeptics. Horne sent employees to visit companies with open offices, like Bloomberg, a maverick in the open-office movement, and Google. He engaged over

25 percent of CBRE employees at all levels to research technology, furniture, culture, health, and what it takes to move to a paperless office.[15] Next, Horne reconfigured a section of the existing office into an experimental zone (think test kitchen) to try out new desks, materials, and computers.

Horne and his team vowed to be transparent and to avoid implementing anything that the senior leaders had not tried first. They documented their experiences and stories in a Friday blog.

Andrew Ratner, a senior leader at CBRE, wrote a blog entry about what it was like to take home the personal items that had been with him in his office for his entire career. During a chat with me, he shared, "After I wrote that, I came home to [my wife], and I showed her all of this cool stuff and she said, 'That's great, here's the garbage. I see it; I don't want it in my house.' You realize that it's just stuff." Then Ratner wrote another post about his feeling upon opening the first file drawer, tasked with either scanning or throwing away the old papers. "You start looking through the files, and you close the drawer . . . you say, I can't do this. And then you eventually have to do it, and you realize . . . 80 percent of what was in there was already on my computer. I came from that era where you didn't trust technology."

Clearly, offering employees like Ratner an opportunity to navigate this process with each other was an important human consideration.

One of the biggest concerns Horne heard was that employees were nervous about getting up to speed on the new procedures and systems. In response, Horne provided training, and lots of it. All employees had access to a personal "digital coach" (a little like your favorite genius at the Apple Store) to set up their computers, migrate their files, and help them learn to live in their new world.[16]

The investment in the "how" seems to have worked.

Since the roll-out, CBRE's Los Angeles office has had over 4,000 visitors come to learn about the process and glean insight into the secret sauce. According to Horne, "The quality of this space has changed our relationship with our employees and has given us an advantage in recruiting talent. Our people love this space, and we've recruited 80 new employees at the downtown office over a two-year period."[17] Not only that, but the new space has also "changed [the] narrative with clients. When we designed this space, we wanted to make it a showroom for our clients."[18]

It's not just clients who are impressed with CBRE's new space. Ratner revealed that people who work there are happier. They're more productive, and they collaborate better.

🤝 HUMAN ACTION PLAN

1. **Align.** As you know by now, I am a big fan of knowing who you are and what your values are. One of the main reasons for this is so that you can actually use your values to develop programs and execute strategies that make sense for your business. Space is a great example. Aligning your space with your values works wonders. One Harvard study found that when researchers, whose mission is to publish and disseminate their findings, sat near each other, their work was cited 45 percent more often![19] It makes sense to put our bodies where our values are.

2. **Change.** Once we get our systems in place, take a deep breath, and change it up. As awesome as it is to have everything lined up and organized, rigidity will always be our ruin. Instead, invite flexibility to keep things fresh and people on their toes. After all, everything is changing anyway, so the more easily your space can respond and adapt to these changes, the better. Get feedback, be open, or maybe even host a Reaping.

3. **Name.** Once you've gone to all that work to line it up and mix it up, you want to be sure people actually use your spaces. One way to lure people in is to give your spaces a name and a narrative. During my visit to CBRE's state-of-the-art Los Angeles office,

detailed earlier, I was introduced to one of my favorite examples of this. CBRE's office is built around what they've identified as "the Heart," a bright, open space with a waiting area, a snack bar, and a concierge who makes sure employees' and guests' needs are being met. For CBRE, the Heart is where the home (office) is. And don't worry, named spaces don't have to be ginormous or particularly noteworthy for the names to come alive. Squarespace, for example, has one little patch of green on the roof that is called "the Hill." And what do you know? On a sunny day, people now say, "Meet me at the Hill."

9

Take Professional Development Personally: Empower Employees to Be Their Best Selves

*One of the things I've realized is when you're
successful, that curiosity that you may have initially
had to build something novel and new gets replaced
by a little bit of, you can call it hubris, I describe
it as the "know-it-all" culture. And we needed to
go from being "know-it-all" to "learn-it-all."*
—SATYA NADELLA, CEO, Microsoft

We used to think of professional development as a
perk we could offer when we were feeling flush, or a
nice-to-have benefit that might help people do their jobs better. A conference here, an off-site there. We hoped that our

investments would pay off in the form of "better" performance over some vague period of time.

In their 2016 *Harvard Business Review* article, authors Michael Beer, Magnus Finnström, and Derek Schrader wrote that development programs, in fact, aren't exactly adding value, that "corporations are victims of the great training robbery," to coin a catchy phrase. They cite that companies spent $160 billion in the United States and close to $356 billion globally on employee training and education in 2015 alone. They explain that "for the most part, the learning doesn't lead to better organizational performance, because people soon revert to their old ways of doing things."[1]

Say goodbye to the foggy, bloated, ill-conceived programs. No matter what you call it—plugging into purpose, creating a "learn-it-all" culture, or simply developing and improving upon good, old-fashioned human resources—strong, human, personal, and professional development is now an absolute must-have.

One of the greatest gifts millennials have given the world is an understanding that human beings need to grow on the job. In fact, "millennials don't just want to spend their time earning a paycheck; they want to invest time acquiring the skills and knowledge they need to grow both personally and professionally."[2] Coincidentally (or not), the most popular course recently offered by Coursera, the online university, was *Learning How to Learn*.[3] I for one believe that this generation is just shining a light on what's good for all of us.

By this I mean the human workplace must take meaningful, on-the-job education seriously, whether it's related to a person's job description or not. Leaders must take it upon themselves to help their employees connect with the right opportunities. Then, instead of focusing on one or maybe two annual conversations, they must build development into the culture, the operations, and the ongoing dialogue, tailoring experiences to actually fit their talent.

At the end of the day, human companies who try to use a one-size-fits-all approach to development won't last. According to Brian Kropp, human resources practice leader at the business advisory firm CEB (now part of Gartner), the lack of career opportunities (i.e., development) is the number one reason employees say they leave an organization, and 70 percent of employees are *dissatisfied* with the growth opportunities at their companies.[4]

How can managers and leaders stay ahead of the game? They can start by offering prized employees a menu of options from old standbys like online classes and in-person workshops. They can bring in outside speakers or offer off-the-wall classes on jewelry making or even on how to launch a company. Managers are learning that inviting a team member's hobby (aka side hustle) or personal obsession into day-to-day operations is not only nothing to fear, it can actually be a boost. The employee feels whole, the team experiences an infusion of passion, and you are likely to retain that employee a little longer—something certainly good for the bottom line. As writer Stephanie Weaver reported in *Inc.*, "Employees with side hustles are often more productive, have characteristics employers want, and think creatively."[5]

Finally, while old-school, top-heavy training can be expensive (and vague), making it personal might cost less than you think and be more valuable than you can imagine.

Go the Extra Mile

In the human workplace, leaders and managers know that one of the best ways to foster an employee's loyalty and engagement is through showing a genuine interest. We can't throw a bunch of professional development options out there and hope people find something that suits them. We need to slow down, pay attention to the individuals on our teams, and make them an offer they can't refuse. Everyone is different and has different needs. Remember, there is no cookie-cutter model to employee engagement!

Aria Finger, the dynamic CEO of DoSomething.org, started at the company in 2005 as an associate. By 2013, she had been promoted four times, reaching the position of chief operating officer, and she was getting a little antsy because she had been with the organization for eight years. She went to her boss, former CEO Nancy Lublin, and expressed what was on her mind. Lublin and Finger had always discussed starting a millennial consulting agency. Finger wrote up the business case, and Lublin agreed 100 percent. Lublin provided the latitude, Finger took the initiative to write up the business case, and Lublin agreed with the conclusions. Lublin knew that to keep a "best athlete" (the term my colleagues and I used for top candidates in my recruiting days) like Finger, she had to allow Finger to spread her wings. Lublin didn't want to see Finger walking out the door with her rock-star talent and years of institutional knowledge. She knew she had to—here it comes—*do something!*

And boy, did she go the extra mile. Lublin gave Finger the blessing to start an agency in-house, right there at DoSomething. She provided the budget to hire an employee and folded this novel idea into the existing business model. And since starting this new firm, TMI (now called DoSomething Strategic), Finger has made sure to encourage growth in her own staff, the way Lublin has always encouraged her.

In order to link up her now 60-person workforce to the development opportunities they so crave, Finger takes it upon herself to keep a running tally of what matters to them. She asks questions like, *What's important to you? Do you want to become a better speaker? Do you want a byline? Do you want a fellowship?* This approach helps her employees feel seen and heard (in fact, they *are* seen *and* heard). DoSomething is a nonprofit, so Finger's training and development cup is not overflowing. She gets a bigger bang for the buck by helping employees build critical skills that are also personally important to them. Everyone wins through Finger's commitment.

For example, Finger was perusing material from a networking group when she learned of a speaking opportunity for a woman of color to talk about women's advocacy and female empowerment. It so happened that Finger's head of engineering had expressed an interest in developing her public speaking skills. Finger made the connection and voilà!—perfectly aligned professional development at your service. Of course, these opportunities don't always have to be so handpicked. For example, Finger's marketing manager recently signed up for a great weekend Google Analytics course, and DoSomething paid for it. What matters is that employees get what they need to grow. Attention to this growth happens to be one of DoSomething's most impressive commitments, something that Finger comes to very, *very*, personally.

Another incredible offering available to all DoSomething employees was actually first handcrafted for Finger by Lublin—the four-week sabbatical. One day, when Finger had been at DoSomething for only about three years, Lublin asked her already star employee straight up if there was a reason she would ever want to leave. Finger answered candidly: "Travel. My friends are traveling around the world. I'm so jealous." Lublin conceived of a solution and responded, "Okay, let's do this," and the sabbatical program was born.

When you or I typically think of a sabbatical, we might think of a 60-year-old, tenured professor who's been teaching for decades. Today, however, staying at a company for even five years amounts to a lifetime in the minds of many workers. In fact, a sabbatical at DoSomething is available for any employee who has been at the company for *two years*. Sounds kind of crazy, but there are a few conditions. First, employees must identify a temporary replacement. The replacement must be someone who can grow both personally and professionally from their new role. Second, before leaving for a sabbatical, the employee must commit to staying at DoSomething for an additional year when they return.

DoSomething sabbaticals take planning. Finding someone internally who is capable of filling in, or even paying someone from the outside to fill in, is challenging at best—especially for the more senior roles. But the peace of mind that comes with knowing Lublin's valued employees return refreshed and evolved is, well, priceless. And effective! More than ten senior-level employees (including Finger herself) have taken sabbaticals since the launch of the program, and they have all stayed with the company for over four years and counting.

Personal development at DoSomething all started with the faith Lublin had in Finger. That faith continued throughout Finger's career. By going the extra mile, this faith was rewarded, as Finger honed the skills to become a CEO, skyrocketing DoSomething to success. Now Finger is in a position to take the same smart gambles, to make the same strategic investments in her "top athletes." And everyone wins big.

SPOTLIGHT
Sidehustle U

Fashion designer Rebecca Minkoff has some seriously lucky employees. Not only is their boss concerned that they "constantly stay inspired and be their own entrepreneurs within their jobs and their life," but she is also willing to invite her own personal contacts in to mentor her staff. "I want my employees to know it's important to take risks and be fearless when wanting to achieve your goals and dreams."

Professional development at its finest . . . and most fashionable.

Make Personal Development Professional at Betterment

Developing relationships is excellent for the bottom line, especially these days. A study by the Addison Group found that millennials are very concerned with making connections at work, not so much for friendship, but for professional development.[6] That's the carrot. There's also a stick. If connections are not established, millennials and other employees will simply leave. The cost of replacing most employees ranges from 10 to 30 percent of their salary, but replacing a highly-skilled key player can cost up to a couple hundred percent of that person's salary![7] No two ways about it: it pays to keep good people on board. *And taking employees' personal development professionally is the winning way to go.*

When Jon Stein was a kid, growing up in Dallas, he was a dedicated Boy Scout. He eventually attained the rank of Eagle Scout, the highest achievement in the Boy Scout program.

Now Stein is the founder and CEO of Betterment, an online investment firm, which has grown at a rate of 300 percent since its start in 2008 and currently manages more than $11 billion in assets. Stein's seven years of scouting showed him the power of being part of a group, and how people working as a team can "move mountains."

As a young Scout, Stein worked to know the people in his patrol. Just as he learned basic skills from his friends, they also learned from him. It's no surprise, then, that as a grown-up CEO, Stein appreciates the impact of keeping all 200 of his employees regularly engaged with each other in a variety of ways. He is so tuned in to honoring relationships (hey, a kindred spirit!) that he believes that meticulously curated connections within the company *are* professional development. It's not that he doesn't also offer the classic skills-enhancement opportunities. But for Stein, the personal *is* professional development. This gut instinct, planted in Stein's early days, has come to guide his work as CEO.

When Stein founded Betterment in 2008, everything from wearing every hat to developing relationships and corporate communication came easily. The left hand always knew what the right hand was doing, everyone knew everyone, and it was easy to flag a problem and connect the dots. As the company grew, departments formed, leading to specialization and less automatic cross-pollination of people and ideas.

Then, in 2012, when Betterment was still at only 50 people, Stein began to perceive a shift in culture. While he realized that specialization and subsequent silo building were a necessary part of their very fast growth (and good news by most accounts), he wanted to retain those healthy connections across the organization. He thought back to his Boy Scout days and began to design a workplace that would foster what mattered most to him.

Today Betterment is a bastion of community cohesion, with a good dose of fun, healthy competition, and the kinds of relationships that do more than make us feel good. Stein is especially fond of mentoring relationships. As Stein puts it, it is good for us to know people "who you want to be when you grow up."

Stein cultivates a philosophy of mentoring that is based on "mentoring availability." As he explained to me, "You want to have someone in a position of power, who you aspire to be more like, and [whom] you can learn from constantly. But you don't want all those relationships to be forced. It should be [something] that people opt into." When I asked him if people on both sides of the mentoring aisle were willing participants, he said, "There are plenty of people who want to be mentors [for] all the people who want to have a mentor relationship." And then, he told me, "you just watch."

Some may view Stein's embrace of mentoring as a personal bias, but research shows that mentoring programs increase workplace productivity. A Gartner study on Sun Microsystems, for example, concluded, "Mentoring has a positive impact on mentors and mentees, producing employees that are more highly valued by the business."[8] Mentors were promoted six times more often than those not in the program; mentees were promoted five times more often than those not in the program; and retention rates were much higher for mentees (72 percent) and mentors (69 percent) than for employees who did not participate in the mentoring program (49 percent).

On a visit to the Betterment offices, I met with two mentor-mentee pairs who were connected through the formal mentorship program. The mentees wanted help "flexing beyond their current role." They wanted to learn to manage up, down, and across the organization, and they wanted someone more senior to "make sense of the craziness" that you get on a fast-moving growth train like Betterment. The mentors opted in, first because they wanted to give back, but also because they loved the fact that they were able to keep their pulse on the growing organization and glean insight into their own management styles.

And guess what? After the conclusion of the two-month formal mentorship program, both pairs I met chose to continue their mentor-mentee relationships. Both have had great successes at work based on these new relationships.

Clearly, Stein is an expert in forging formal relationships. But he also knows that learning can come from places where we least expect it. Recalling what he learned about the number eight from his days as a Boy Scout ("it's the optimal number to be able to build relationships"), Stein created eight-person Betterment "bands," a way for the company "to retain some of the benefits of being smaller, closer, and tighter-knit."

This is how it works. Every employee is assigned to a cross-functional group, ideally with one person from each Betterment department, with a budget for outings and monthly lunches always served with a side helping of competition—a trivia contest or bingo game—to keep things lively. The bands are encouraged to build intra-band relationships through these monthly events, and the members sit together at work for a given time frame ranging from a year to two years and sometimes longer. To show the importance of the bands, they are outlined in the company handbook, *The Betterment Way*: "It's fun. It's team-building. It's also temporary. Every so often, the bands get shuffled, and everyone is assigned to a new group of people. New hires hang out with veterans, sales folks hang out with designers, ideas get shared, disciplines cross-pollinate, and all sorts of good things happen."[9]

In addition to all of these opportunities to be social, to compete, and to connect, Betterment also offers a whole host of other professional development opportunities. Employees and outside experts teach classes on general topics like how to manage up and how to deal with conflict, and in more straight-forward areas like finance and operations. Moreover, employees are encouraged to participate in Betterment University on particular days when a stream of classes is available for everyone.

At Betterment, when evaluating progress, end-of-year performance reviews are more an opportunity to provide feedback about an employee's chosen career trajectory than the old-school critique. Extended reviews happen twice a year (in the fall and the spring) and are taken very seriously, as a way of explicitly supporting the growth of the Betterment workforce both professionally and personally.

Stein's intentional commitment to honoring relationships in all these ways makes him a human hero in my book (figuratively and literally!). After all, this is his motto: *Small Teams, Full Hearts, Can't Lose.*

I couldn't agree more.

Stein has made professional development better. And, more personal.

SPOTLIGHT

The Book Club

Nathan Rosenberg, CEO of Insigniam (a "break-through management consulting firm" based in

Laguna Beach, California), started a book club where all of his 65 employees read and discuss two books a year. "I love walking around the office and seeing people of all levels, of all functions, huddled into corners of the office talking about the book."

Rosenberg chooses books he believes will provide lessons and learning his employees can apply to their jobs and ones that will lead to provocative conversations among colleagues. His two most recent selections were *Atlas Shrugged* by Ayn Rand and *Getting Naked,* a management book by Patrick Lencioni.

Connecting and learning through reading. A novel idea?!

Express Yourselves Through Self-Discovery

Human beings are creative creatures, but that doesn't necessarily mean we all love to paint, dance, or write poetry. Our very nature is creative, which is how we innovate, problem solve, and collaborate. And it's also how we learn to self-reflect, which is an integral part of the human workplace. Bringing a creative spirit to training and professional development isn't just good for people who might ordinarily be drawn to such endeavors though. It can introduce *everyone* to new types of awareness, which is both good for people and great for business.

Refinery29 describes itself as "the leading global media company focused on young women." Reaching 550 million women around the world,[10] they aim to empower and amplify women's lives through personal narratives, fresh content, and boundless creativity. Therefore, it wasn't a big surprise when I learned that Refinery29's professional development philosophy focuses less on conventional workplace skills (such as how to "manage" others) than on how to deepen relationships and manage oneself. This is a team on a serious quest to bring their very best humans to work.

I had the pleasure of speaking with Refinery29's chief people officer, Carolyn Meacher, about what she refers to as Refinery29's "learning mindset." She explained to me, "We believe in the idea of self-awareness and self-management and people really showing up in a responsible way," which clearly guides how Refinery29 approaches its learning and development. Meacher continued, "Rather than doing a lot of technical leadership training around skills such as how do you do a performance review, we focus on empathy, strength spotting, self-awareness, and self-management, so that people can show up more authentically and not try to hide from problems."

Putting their money where their mouth is, Refinery29 invested in training 70 of their top leaders in emotional intelligence and empathy, and the result has been "outstanding." After the training, these leaders felt that they had a "new awareness around the environment they create at work [and] how they connect with peers and the people who work with them." They were so pleased to begin this process of self-discovery that they wanted more. After noticing aspects about themselves that made their jobs more difficult, such as their anger, frustration, or impatience, "they want[ed] coaching around how they could change those behaviors."

Meacher, a certified coach, and her team were happy to oblige. She does a lot of the coaching herself, and Refinery29 has hired a crew of outside coaches for "either somebody who's been put into a new stretch role or somebody who might be struggling . . . or . . . somebody who has a large span of control . . . who's never had any learning or individualized attention in terms of their leadership skills." When I asked for an example of how coaching helped smooth out a situation, she had this story at the ready:

> We hired somebody starting in a new role from an outside company, and she was starting with a team that was not open to having a new leader. The leader who had recently left was beloved and it would have been a tough situation for any new manager. [In the coaching], first of all, the manager learned how to be much more aware of her personal strengths and styles . . . and how those might be felt by the team. Second, through the coaching she learned some practical tools around how [to] build those relationships when she was not necessarily being welcomed with open arms.

And now?

> On both sides . . . of the table [there has] just been remarkable change and here we are a year later and the team is in a totally different place. It's really cohesive. The relationships are completely solid. The leader has established herself as a really trusted, motivated, [and] motivating inspirational leader.

Individual coaching can carry a pretty steep price tag, but you'll ultimately lose more time and money finding replacements if you don't invest in the employees you have. As Meacher puts it, "I think about the ROI and just being able to retain one person on that team that might have left if it didn't work out with that manager. This whole thing pays for itself."

In addition to helping employees delve deeply into their own tendencies and behavior in order to bring their most genuine self to work, Refinery29 encourages light, easy, and fun modes of creative expression. As part of its Academy, which hosts speakers, lunch-and-learns, and the like, they also have the School of Self-Expression. The School offers classes such as collage making (the day I visited they were having a class with over 30 people), storytelling, and paper marbling. These classes are popular and usually "sell out." Employees get to meet people from other parts of the company, and the leaders make sure that people are mixing it up by sitting with colleagues they don't know. The classes are meditative in nature and help employees decompress at the end of the day. As a bonus, because they are creating content 24/7 at Refinery29, they can take photographs of the art for use on their site.

Refinery29's approach to creative, personal professional development is truly ahead of the curve. As Meacher put it so well, "The way I see it is it doesn't matter how strong somebody's technical skills are if they can't manage relationships. If they can't manage stress, if they're operating from a place of fear . . . it doesn't matter what their technical skills are because they won't be able to access them. They won't be able to put them in play."

A person who knows how to manage relationships, including the important relationship with one's self, is also able to honor those relationships. A person like that can bring her or his human to work.

The positive effects of deeply personal professional development are difficult to overstate. Committing to one's valuable talent, bringing people together in productive social groups, and mining for creative self-expression are all ways of bringing out the best in people. Regardless of industry or approach, from a human point of view, the personal and the professional are deeply intertwined. When we understand this connection, we can really make a difference in our productivity and in people's lives.

SPOTLIGHT

Do, Model, Coach, Enable

SYPartners, a leadership consulting firm with the tagline "The human side of transformation," is committed to helping its employees develop in ways that are critical to personal growth. When an employee first joins the firm, gets started on a new project, or is promoted to a new role, she meets with her manager in a meeting called Do, Model, Coach, Enable. In this meeting, the manager helps identify where the employee feels confident jumping in and where more coaching might be needed. From these sorts of meetings, a "social contract" is written, whereby employees are committed to supporting someone else through their learning curve. Both mentor and mentee advance their knowledge, wisdom, and, yes, of course, their relationship.

🤝 HUMAN ACTION PLAN

1. **Ask.** We have seen that growth and development are a critical part of creating a human workplace. And without it, you will have trouble retaining your people. So how do we get started? Just ask your people what they want! Ask employees what they want to learn and how they want to learn it. If they aren't sure, they will be thrilled to give it some thought and get back to you. Millennials and Gen Z want to bring their whole selves to work, so why not provide opportunities for them to do just that? They'll be happier and they'll stick around longer, too.

2. **Receive.** Your employees are doing cool things after work. I guarantee it. Your very own workforce is an untapped wealth of knowledge, skills, and insights that other people in your company will no doubt enjoy. After asking employees how they themselves want to develop (see above), try asking them what they'd like to offer to their colleagues. Taking classes is one way to gain important skills, and teaching classes is another. By trading knowledge, you are creating a network of people all taking their professional development personally—together.

3. **Coach.** More and more companies are offering coaching to employees at every stage in their career. When people become leaders, or parents, or find themselves in a new position, the

overwhelming fear can cost the individual and the company. So it just makes sense to offer people support along the way. While it might seem counterintuitive to offer coaching to employees who already seem qualified for their jobs, offering additional support says, "I care about you and your happiness." Having truly happy, actualized people on your staff is a great retention strategy. And coaching helps every employee develop—professionally and personally.

10

Say Thank You: It's a Human Thing to Do

first met Ashley Peterson, a barista at my local New York City Starbucks, just over six years ago during my morning ritual—stopping in for a grande, extra-hot soy latte while taking my three kids to school and my very human self to work. Ashley's big, warm smile was always a comfort to me in the midst of my morning wrangle. Ashley always seemed to mean it when she looked us in the eyes and asked, "How is everyone today?"

It wasn't long before Ashley learned all of our names, our go-to drinks, and our favorite breakfast treats. One fall, my daughter Caroline developed a taste (read: obsession) for Starbucks' pumpkin scones. Caroline was devastated when Ashley explained that the scones disappear shortly after Halloween. Every time we stopped in, we would ask Ashley how many pumpkin scones were left and order more than our fair share, until finally, about a week or so after Halloween, Caroline ate her last one of the season.

On our next visit, I grabbed my coffee and we Keswins continued our walk down Broadway. Suddenly, I heard my name being called. I looked back and saw my Starbucks friend, Ashley, running down the crowded sidewalk toward us. I thought maybe I had forgotten to pay (in an era before my handy app handled my transaction). I also recall wondering if she was okay. After Ashley met up with us and caught her breath, she handed Caroline a bag with a piece of gingerbread in it, saying that since she loves pumpkin, she might like the gingerbread, too.

Somewhat stunned by her kindness (this was New York City, remember), we thanked Ashley, accepted the bag with the gingerbread in it, and continued our walk to school, smiling on the inside. As it turns out, Caroline does not like gingerbread. But that's not all I learned that day.

Ashley's completely off-script, surprise gesture of thoughtfulness stayed with me. It was so personal, it was so . . . real. As a customer, I was touched; I felt seen, special, and appreciated, like my many years of Starbucks devotion was being reciprocated. As a workplace strategist, I was blown away. I saw firsthand what it looks like for someone to really care about her work.

That's when I started thinking . . . if only Starbucks could bottle Ashley's magic. If only we could all be so truly and honestly connected to the work we do. If only we could all bring our human to work.

That sidewalk rendezvous with Ashley was the inspiration for this book. I wanted to learn more about why and how this young woman took her work to heart. I knew that this passion was important to our connection to work as employees and employers, to our personal lives, and to our bottom line. It's important to making our work lives feel as though they have meaning. So I wanted to understand how we can all be a little more like Ashley.

Just as we began this human work narrative with values, so shall we end. Ashley lives the Starbucks values.

As I experienced personally, Ashley believes in "treating customers like family" by making her delivery of customer service the best she can. How? There's a Starbucks barista adage that goes, "Love it or let me know." And Ashley, to the core of her being, wants everybody who comes into Starbucks to leave happy.

One surefire way to make people happy is to infuse gratitude into their day-to-day life. Harvard University cites research that has linked the act of being grateful with increased happiness.[1] Ashley does this by thanking her customers each day, explicitly of course. But also—and more powerfully in my opinion—she implicitly says, *I know you*, and I appreciate your business, personally.

Howard Schultz, Starbucks' longtime CEO, says: "Our role as leaders is to celebrate the human connection that we have been able to create as a company, and to make sure people realize the deep level of respect we have for the work they do. . . . That is the legacy of the company."

This attitude of offering recognition to its employees is real.

Ashley has been promoted three times since I first met her. First she moved to a local Starbucks, farther uptown. Then she headed over to the East Side, where she was the assistant store manager at a new Starbucks Reserve store on 84th Street and Madison Avenue. Most recently, she reached her goal of managing her own store. Manhattanites all up and down Broadway have changed their morning migration patterns to get their morning fix from Ashley.

As both Howard Schultz and Ashley Peterson realize, we all like to be recognized. This includes simple customers like me. Just look at what that scone incident has engendered—allegiance, a deep relationship, genuine respect. This book.

Yet, as much as we might wish to be, we can't all be Ashleys, with compassion and charisma to spare. Nor do we need to be. Human businesses are truly diverse (and should be! See Chapter Two). Even if we're not Ashley-like in personality, there are still plenty of opportunities to bring our human to work. Learning how to express gratitude is a great place to start.

Of course, I am neither the first nor the only person to appreciate the power of gratitude. The question of "how to be grateful" is so big these days that an entire industry has sprung up. Globoforce is a successful company devoted to helping companies (some of which are profiled in this book) find their own way of expressing gratitude. Saying thank you is the right thing to do, and just as Globoforce's CEO Eric Mosley makes clear, "The simple act of recognizing employees has a proven impact on your bottom line."

In this concluding chapter, I share stories from powerhouse brands that honor relationships by putting gratitude to work. It's a critical topic (aren't they all?), and I have broken it down by Who, When, and How.

WHO: Everyone Can #Soulitforward

Offering gratitude is everyone's job. Receiving it should be everyone's opportunity. Yes, gratitude is a two-way street. Leaders and managers should aim to dole out thanks on a regular basis. Peers can thank peers. Customers can be encouraged to thank team members. Great clients always love thank-yous, and what's the downside to thanking your boss?

SoulCycle is a high-energy brand if there ever was one. With over 20,000 riders on their spin bikes each week, the company is opening 10 to 15 new studios a year.[2] Whatever they're doing, it's working. The brand is now synonymous with life-affirming self-care through hard work—move over, apple pie! SoulCycle is an icon of the American spirit of today.

Beloved by biking enthusiasts from Michelle Obama to Lady Gaga to David Beckham, SoulCycle has earned the cult-like loyalty of people who aspire to a fierce, mega-inspiring life. Melanie Whelan, SoulCycle's CEO, and a woman after my own heart who's committed to weaving the company's values into everything she does, is exactly the type of person her company attracts. One of SoulCycle's values is "show gratitude," a humble expression coming from such a super-success. SoulCycle defines gratitude as *We give thanks to our riders, our staff, and each other. We are humble and remember it takes a village.*

Whelan and her employees express gratitude in many ways, but one of my favorites is their very cool (and contagious) pin program. Employees are "gifted" a package of pins after a year with the company, with each pin representing one of Soul-Cycle's 10 core values. There's a We Get Dirty pin (i.e., every single employee is responsible for the day-to-day operations), a Culture of Yes pin (i.e., everyone is committed to saying "yes" to riders and doing whatever it takes to satisfy their desires), and an Embrace Change pin.

When an employee sees anyone embodying any of the company's values, he or she is encouraged to #Soulitforward—give the person a pin, and *share* with the recipient how the actions were inspiring and emblematic of the values. Giving thanks in this systematic way creates what Whelan described as "an ecosystem of celebration of core values." Every leader would do well to consider how they might create just such an ecosystem.[3]

Because of this values-laden environment, the SoulCycle pins have become hot collector's items, and top recipients have become "legends."[4] Rudy Volcy, one such legend, is a facilities manager and has received 17 pins to date. Volcy remembers receiving his first pin. "It was from [someone] in the legal department. . . . She wanted me to know that she noticed and appreciated the hard work that goes into keeping this office looking its best. Each one of those pins keeps me motivated and wanting to work harder."

One of the best parts about Volcy's story is that he feels he is not "just" the facilities manager; he is a devoted brand ambassador. He says, "These pins just tell me that we all play a crucial part in keeping the machine moving, regardless of title. We all have an impact on this brand and how people view our brand, so let's represent with integrity."[5]

Whelan's attention to values is not incidental, or a mere "nice to have." Not even close. In an interview with *Fast Company,* Wheelan talked about the power of bringing these core values to life: "[Using the pins] is how we've been able to scale [our culture]."[6]

As Whelan and her team continue their ambitious plan fueled by a steady dose of high-octane gratitude, we should all take note, and recognize that people at every level of our organization, in every kind of job, can take a moment, look around, and see who deserves thanks and for what. Then give it.

WHEN: Every Morning at 9 a.m.

The old-school routine of only offering thanks (and any feedback, for that matter) at the end of the year, during the annual performance reviews, is becoming just as obsolete as those pink While You Were Out message pads.

This change comes not a moment too soon, if you ask me!

Nowadays, if you wait until that one intimidating meeting that occurs once a year to provide feedback, or wait until your employees' work anniversaries to say thank you, you will likely have missed the proverbial boat, and you might find that your best workers have already moved on. Instead, it's important to infuse your calendar with a culture of gratitude. This can be done in a variety of ways—by establishing regular feedback sessions and by developing good daily habits.

Indagare, a boutique, membership-based, travel community founded in 2007 by Melissa Biggs Bradley (Indagare's CEO) and Eliza Harris (Indagare's COO), is named after the Latin word meaning seek, discover, or scout. The two women had worked together at *Town & Country Travel* magazine and bonded as new moms who also wanted to have meaningful professional careers.

Since the two founders came from the editorial world, Indagare began as a place where members received curated content. Members quickly became part of a community of people who were passionate about the world of travel. Biggs Bradley and Harris believed that if people felt that they were part of a community, they would be more likely to have open and honest discussions about better ways to travel, which would lead to "transformative journeys and meaningful global connections." Indagare's members loved the content, but what they really craved was help in planning amazing trips with top-notch service.

Biggs Bradley and Harris shared a passion for creating a workplace where they and their 75 employees could be their best selves at work, ready to manage the stresses that come with the job. Between weather delays, flight cancellations, and lost luggage, frustration levels are often high in the travel world. Moreover, the "discerning" travel business has its own unique brand of stress. Clients are paying top dollar and expect an awful lot from their advisors. Sometimes they even expect their advisors to predict and control the weather!

Harris, Biggs Bradley, and the company's director of people and culture, Shoshana Balistierri, are responsible for scaling the culture (not an easy job, especially during periods of high growth). Harris recently spoke to me about a book she read describing how the act of wishing happiness on another person was, in and of itself, something that made the well-wisher happier and uplifted. Harris decided to give this happiness wishing a whirl.

Thanks to the advice Harris gleaned from this book, Indagare holds regular, *daily* gratitude sessions. "At 9 a.m., we grab whoever is around for our morning gratitude practice." The folks at Indagare take turns around the room, as each person is invited to offer one thing for which they are grateful and one wish of happiness to another person. As Harris conveyed, "What we've discovered is it's the most delightful way to start the day when you see how people's faces light up when they're saying what they're grateful for." Knowing what we know about the science of gratitude, and how good happiness is for productivity and creativity, this is to be expected. But there's more.

Harris and her employees found that giving and receiving gratitude had become a wonderful way to get to know each other. "When you hear the specifics of what people in our office are grateful for, you really start to get to know your colleagues and what's going on in their lives in an authentic, non-intrusive way."

For the truly human manager, this kind of insight is golden. What better way to honor relationships than to actually listen in on what's happening in people's lives and to reciprocate?

A practice like the Indagare gratitude circle is good for people, especially people who are working so closely with high-stakes stress every day. It's also good for business. We all know that millennials (actually all people) want more connection, more feedback, and more meaningful relationships. As they should! A Gallup study shows that having a best friend at work—someone at work you can really talk to—correlates with higher engagement and lower attrition.[7]

A regular, daily cup of gratitude can teach us a lot about ourselves and our colleagues.

HOW: Lift Employees to New Heights (35,000 Feet)

JetBlue manages to safely shuttle over 38 million people from one place to another every year. Pretty impressive! But customers aren't the only ones getting a lift from JetBlue. Employees also get a "lift" that comes in the form of recognition for a job well done.

In fact, one of the many reasons I love JetBlue is that they take their culture as seriously as anything, except perhaps, understandably, their flights. JetBlue's Lift program is no exception. The program is powered by Globoforce, the gratitude gurus I referenced earlier in the chapter. To begin, JetBlue aligns its gratitude program with its company values, an idea I highly recommend. What could be better than making people feel good and emphasizing core values at the same time?

At JetBlue, when crew members feel inspired, they can nominate one of their peers, their direct reports, or even their boss for upholding the JetBlue values in some remarkable way. The person nominated is rewarded immediately with a gift card of their choice. The key to this program is saying thank you in real time. Employees don't have to wait six months or even a week for some type of formal discussion. Within four months of adopting the program, employees felt more appreciated by 88 percent. Amazing!

One encouraging Lift story comes from LaToya Jordan, JetBlue's director of talent management and diversity. She was working at the airport when there was a delay. A long delay. She witnessed a crew member handling the situation with "grace, a sense of calm, and even a little bit of levity." At the end of the delay, as people were getting ready to board, this crew member acknowledged over the PA that they had all been there for a long time and suggested that everyone look around to ensure they hadn't left anything behind, as phones had been plugged in all around the boarding gate.

As Jordan recounted, "I saw the crowd nod their heads and say 'Oh yeah.' It was just a friendly reminder, but he did it in such a nice and helpful way and walked around and talked to people. So, I sent him a Lift. He didn't know I was watching. He was just doing what came naturally, living the JetBlue values. But saying thank you allowed me/JetBlue to recognize the crew member and reinforce those values."

Yet another great Lift story comes from Rachel McCarthy, who is part of JetBlue's people team. Previously, she worked at the company in marketing and in-flight operations. She told me a remarkable story of a Lift-worthy moment that occurred while she was there:

> *A crew member orchestrated a faux pre-wedding for a couple on their way to get married. As this crew member sang and performed the ceremony, another carried napkins that were turned into a floral display. A third served as a witness. This JetBlue experience even included a passenger who happened to have a violin with him and people danced in the aisles. The whole plane was whooping and hollering and having fun.*

At JetBlue, fun is clearly serious business. After all, fun is #5 on JetBlue's list of core values. McCarthy sent the entire flight team a Lift to say "thank you for being you."

Nothing in the employee handbook teaches someone how to get on the PA, or sing and help celebrate a happy moment. But saying thank you and giving the crew members a "Lift" reinforced JetBlue's values and made it clear that living them is recognized and even rewarded.

All this thanks-giving is not some new-age gimmick to trick people into feeling good. Science and data show that it pays to direct our attention to the power of gratitude. For instance, acclaimed Wharton professor and bestselling author Adam Grant worked with JetBlue to analyze the data from the Lift program. Grant and his team of grad students learned that employee engagement scores not only improved for the people who received recognition, but also for those who gave it. A win-win! And another study out of the University of Birmingham reported that, "the list of potential benefits of gratitude is almost endless: fewer intellectual biases, more effective learning strategies, more helpfulness towards others, raised self-confidence, better work attitude, strengthened resiliency, less physical pain, improved health, and longevity."[8]

And finally, a *Harvard Business Review* article found that "too many companies bet on having a cut-throat, high-pressure, take-no-prisoners culture to drive their financial success."[9] But in truth, everything, including the bottom line, improves with gratitude.

One day not long ago, I found myself on the Upper East Side and decided to pop into Starbucks for a latte and to visit my barista friend, Ashley. I told Ashley that I was heading to Aspen, Colorado, and that Howard Schultz, Starbucks' longtime CEO, was going to be a keynote speaker at an event I was planning to attend. Since I have known Ashley, my respect for her has only grown. I have felt grateful, in fact, to have had this relationship with her. I felt honored to have shared in her incredible personal story and to have basked in the gratitude she expresses for the opportunities Starbucks has provided for her and her daughter. In the moment, I offered to hand Howard Schultz a letter, if she wanted to write one.

Of course, Ashley being Ashley, she did.

Hi Howard,

> *My name is Ashley Peterson and I've been a partner for six years. I recently got a promotion to become a store manager, which I'm really excited about. When I first started at Starbucks, it was just a job for me. Before my Starbucks career, I was on my way to college, but life happened. I was expecting a child, my daughter Mckenzie, who is now five years old. Within a year of being at 81st & Broadway, I knew that Starbucks was for me. With so much I can write, I just want to thank you. Thank you for sharing such a great company with me. Thank you for allowing me to provide for my child. Thank you for the opportunity to work for Starbucks. I will continue to inspire and nurture the human spirit, one person, one cup, one neighborhood at a time.*

Ashley Peterson

Perhaps some of us might feel uncomfortable expressing such gratitude to anyone, let alone the CEO of a multinational corporation. But for Ashley, whose first job in the food industry was as a manager at White Castle when she was 15, this was natural. This young woman has a lot to teach us all about the meaning of hard work and the power of human connection.

According to a survey of 2,000 Americans by the John Templeton Foundation, the workplace ranked as the least likely place for people to express or feel gratitude.[10] Most agreed that saying "thank you" to colleagues makes them "feel happier and more fulfilled," yet only 10 percent did this regularly, and a full 60 percent reported never having said "thank you" or only saying so once a year.

It seems so simple. We should all do it. Every day. However we can. Just say thank you.

It's good for people, great for business, and just might change the world.

HUMAN ACTION PLAN

A human workplace is one where there is a culture of recognizing people and saying I know and appreciate you. The key to creating this culture of gratitude is thinking about how, when, and to whom you are saying thank you.

1. **Who?** Everyone. Creating a culture of gratitude is not only about a manager thanking his or her employees for doing their jobs. Peers can thank peers. Employees can thank their managers. Clients and business partners can be shown appreciation for their business. "The Hershey Company enables 13,000 employees around the globe to recognize and thank people for great performance anytime, anywhere, using a computer or a mobile app."[11] Once the culture of gratitude gets rolling, there's no stopping it.

2. **When?** Often. People want feedback, and they want it on a regular basis—especially millennials and Gen Z. Even if your company is sticking with the year-end reviews (I know, I know . . . old habits die hard), you can offer thanks throughout the year. Or, like Indagare does, at 9 a.m. every morning. I attended one of Investopedia's all-hands meetings, and CEO David Siegel started the weekly meeting by calling out and thanking people for their work on specific projects. I felt grateful just being there!

3. **How?** Make it personal. And make it real. The best thank-yous are ones that highlight something specific that has been done on a project, or a way that someone made you feel. Take the time to find out how your employees have impacted others in very specific ways and then tell them about it. The Muse has a "shout-out board" where people can write and leave notes that thank other employees for something they have done.

ACKNOWLEDGMENTS

This book is about honoring relationships, and I am grateful for the many, many incredible relationships that have shaped my career from early on and that persist to this day.

Howard Levine of Mercer and Jim Bagley of Russell Reynolds Associates taught me what it means to be a good manager and allowed me to bring my human to work. Sherry Turkle of MIT inspired me to find a way to manage my obsession with technology and to ask the right questions.

I am very grateful to my agent, Jane Dystel, who pushed me to get my ideas down on paper, and to my sister, Lauren Rutkin, and my brother-in-law, Rabbi Matthew Gewirtz, for the warm introduction to Jane. My editor at McGraw-Hill, Amy Li, really connected with the material in the book, helped bring it to life, and appreciated that this material is not just for companies, but also for humans looking for a place to work. Thank you to the rest of the McGraw-Hill team—Donya Dickerson, Chelsea Van Der Gaag, Nora Hennick, Maureen Harper, and Daina Penikas—for your support in marketing and production.

I'd like to give thanks to my Spaghetti Project team, starting with Bethany Saltman, brand strategist, collaborator, editor, life coach, and friend. Your wisdom and guidance to "trust the force" wasn't always easy to hear, but you were right! Alexa Clements, thank you for your flexibility, for always being willing to roll up your sleeves and do whatever was needed, and for always staying focused on the details.

Thank you to David Gee for designing my amazing book cover and for working through its many iterations. And a shout-out to Eric Gordon and Steve Koester for their excellent attention to detail with all things design and digital.

I am grateful to JConnelly, Inc. and Dee Dee DeBartlo, whose insights into the issues covered in the book have helped me deepen my connections and widen my impact. Thank you!

To my readers, Jennifer Schiff, Jill Weiss, and Amy Yenkin—thank you for dedicating hours and hours to read and provide detailed feedback on the book. Your changes are appreciated and have been incorporated, and your friendship is uplifting.

To the many people who supported me and my work, investing their time, energy, and expertise to bring this project to life. Randi Friedman, Alison Heisler, Robin Kranich, Susan McPherson, Pam Mittman, David Ryan Polgar, Bobbi Rebell, Barbara Reich, Dayna Spitz, Andrew Stern, Shelley Zalis, and Randi Zuckerberg—thank you! Thank you to the women of TheLi.st who provide ongoing encouragement and support—what an amazing community! I feel very lucky to be a part of it.

And to my family. First, to my husband, Jeff—you are my biggest cheerleader, and of course, detail-oriented proofreader. I have learned so much from you and your ability to connect with people. We make an amazing human team!

Finally, thank you to Julia, Caroline, and Daniel, who have taught me so much about life and love. You are my sweet spot. Thank you for letting me test out my theories on you and for cutting me a little slack while I worked on this book and missed a hockey game and a ski race or two, and sent Daniel to basketball tryouts on the wrong weekend! This book is ultimately for you. I hope that you bring your human to everything you do.

NOTES

INTRODUCTION
1. *Big Demands and High Expectations: The Deloitte Millennial Survey.* United Kingdom: DTTL Global Brand & Communications, 2014. Accessed June 19, 2018. https://www2.deloitte.com/content /dam/Deloitte/global/Documents/About-Deloitte/gx-dttl-2014 -millennial-survey-report.pdf.
2. "Workplace Stress." The American Institute of Stress. Accessed January 15, 2018. https://www.stress.org/workplace-stress/.

CHAPTER 1
1. *Big Demands and High Expectations: The Deloitte Millennial Survey.* United Kingdom: DTTL Global Brand & Communications, 2014. Accessed June 19, 2018. https://www2.deloitte.com/content /dam/Deloitte/global/Documents/About-Deloitte/gx-dttl-2014 -millennial-survey-report.pdf.
2. Cable, Daniel M., Francesca Gino, and Bradley R. Staats. "Breaking Them in or Eliciting Their Best? Reframing Socialization Around Newcomers' Authentic Self-expression." *Administrative Science Quarterly* 58, no. 1 (2013): 1–36, doi:10 .1177/0001839213477098.
3. Downie, Ryan. "What's Behind JetBlu's 63.5% Rise in 10 Years? (JBLU)." Investopedia. August 11, 2016. https://www .investopedia.com/articles/markets/081116/whats-behind-jetblus -635-rise-10-years-jblu.asp.
4. Clune, Bronwen. "How Airbnb Is Building Its Culture Through Belonging." Culture Amp Blog. Accessed January 15, 2018. https://blog.cultureamp.com/how-airbnb-is-building-its-culture -through-belonging.
5. Dani, Anurag. "Basic Differences Between Uber and Lyft." Medium. January 17, 2016. https://medium.com/@Anurag501 /basic-differences-between-uber-and-lyft-100f9fd1fba.

CHAPTER 2
1. "Mission-Driven Sustainability." *Harvard Business Review.* Accessed January 15, 2018. https://hbr.org/2017/12/the-future -economy-project-qa-with-marne-levine.

2. Urist, Jacoba. "What the Marshmallow Test Really Teaches About Self-Control." *Atlantic*. September 24, 2014. https://www .theatlantic.com/health/archive/2014/09/what-the-marshmallow -test-really-teaches-about-self-control/380673/.

3. Koloc, Nathaniel. "What Job Candidates Really Want: Meaningful Work." *Harvard Business Review*. August 7, 2014. https://hbr.org /2013/04/what-job-candidates-really-wan.

4. Hsu, Tiffany. "Microsoft CEO Says Tech's Progress on Gender Equality Is 'Not Sufficient.'" *New York Times*. September 26, 2017. https://www.nytimes.com/2017/09/26/business/satya-nadella -microsoft-gender-equality.html

5. Nadella, Satya. "Satya Nadella: The C in CEO Stands for Culture." *Fast Company*. October 10, 2017. https://www.fastcompany.com /40457741/satya-nadella-the-c-in-ceo-stands-for-culture.

6. Lamach, Michael W. "How Our Company Connected Our Strategy to Sustainability Goals." *Harvard Business Review*. October 30, 2017. https://hbr.org/2017/10/how-our-company -connected-our-strategy-to-sustainability-goals.

7. Schwantes, Marcel. "What Do Millennials Want from Their Employers, Exactly? This Study Sums It Up in 1 Sentence." Inc. com. April 19, 2017. https://www.inc.com/marcel-schwantes /what-do-millennials-want-from-their-employers-exactly-this -study-sums-it-up-in-1.html.

8. Schwantes, Marcel. "Science Found the 5 Things That Drive Employees to Go Above and Beyond." Inc.com. April 19, 2017. https://www.inc.com/marcel-schwantes/the-science-behind-what -really-drives-employee-happiness-it-may-surprise-you.html.

9. Franco, Henry. "HubSpot Named a Best Workplace for Flexibility by Fortune and Great Place to Work." HubSpot. March 29, 2016. https://www.hubspot.com/company-news/hubspot-named-a-best -workplace-for-flexibility-by-fortune-and-great-place-to-work.

10. Jenkin, Matthew. "Babies at Work: Will Onsite Childcare Become Standard in Offices?" *Guardian*. January 13, 2016. https://www .theguardian.com/sustainable-business/2016/jan/13/babies-at -work-onsite-childcare-office-goldman-sachs-addison-lee.

11. Bellis, Rich. "Patagonia's CEO Explains How to Make On-Site Child Care Pay for Itself." *Fast Company*. March 7, 2017. https:// www.fastcompany.com/3062792/patagonias-ceo-explains-how -to-make-onsite-child-care-pay-for-itself.

12. Bellis. "Make On-Site Child Care Pay for Itself."

13. *Tackling Childcare: The Business Case for Employer-Supported Childcare*. Report. September 2017. https://iwpr.org/wp-content /uploads/2017/10/IFC_Tackling-Childcare_Business-Case-for -Employer-Supported-Childcare.pdf.

14. Galatro, Marina A. "HR Corner: Bereavement Leave." Willis Towers Watson. February 8, 2017. Accessed January 16, 2018. https://www.willistowerswatson.com/en/insights/2017/02/hr -corner-bereavement-leave.

15. Van Giezen, Robert W. "Employer Costs for Employee Compensation." U.S. Bureau of Labor Statistics. August 2013. https://www.bls.gov/opub/btn/volume-2/paid-leave-in-private-industry-over-the-past-20-years.htm.

16. Bridges, Frances. "Sheryl Sandberg on How to Help a Grieving Loved One This Holiday Season." *Forbes*. November 30, 2017. https://www.forbes.com/sites/francesbridges/2017/11/30/sheryl-sandbergs-advice-for-how-to-help-a-grieving-loved-one-this-holiday-season/#73f79b86107e.

17. Vyas, Vani. "Mastercard Extends Its Bereavement Leave Policy to 20 Days." People Matters. June 22, 2017. https://www.peoplematters.in/news/compensation-benefits/mastercard-extends-its-bereavement-leave-policy-to-20-days-15729.

18. Grant, Adam. "How to Trust People You Don't Like" and "Faking Your Emotions at Work." *WorkLife with Adam Grant*. Podcast audio, March 28 and April 4, 2018. https://itunes.apple.com/us/podcast/worklife-with-adam-grant/id1346314086?mt=2.

19. Levine, Sheen S., Evan P. Apfelbaum, Mark Bernard, Valerie L. Bartelt, Edward J. Zajac, and David Stark. "Ethnic Diversity Deflates Price Bubbles." *Proceedings of the National Academy of Sciences of the United States of America* 111, no. 52 (November 17, 2014): 18524-18529. Accessed July 5, 2017. doi:10.1073/pnas.1407301111.

20. Kauflin, Jeff. "Committing To Diversity From Day One: A Founder's Story." Forbes. 22 May 2017. https://www.forbes.com/sites/jeffkauflin/2017/05/22/diversity-in-the-founding-team-is-a-key-to-success-for-this-silicon-valley-entrepreneur/#330b8bb407d4

21. McKinsey & Company. *Women Matter 2*. McKinsey & Company, 2008. https://www.mckinsey.de/files/Women_Matter_2_brochure.pdf.

22. Flood, Aoife. *The PwC Diversity Journey: Creating Impact, Achieving Results*. Report. September 2016. https://www.pwc.com/gx/en/diversity-inclusion/best-practices/assets/the-pwc-diversity-journey.pdf.

23. "DiversityInc Announces 2017 Top 50 Companies for Diversity List." PR Newswire. May 3, 2017. https://www.prnewswire.com/news-releases/diversityinc-announces-2017-top-50-companies-for-diversity-list-300450767.html.

24. Hong, Lu, and Scott E. Page. "Groups of Diverse Problem Solvers Can Outperform Groups of High-Ability Problem Solvers." *Proceedings of the National Academy of Sciences of the United States of America*, 101, no. 46 (November 8, 2004): 16385-16389. Accessed January 16, 2018. doi:10.1073/pnas.0403723101.

25. Forbes Insights. *Global Diversity and Inclusion: Fostering Innovation Through a Diverse Workforce*. Report. Accessed January 16, 2018. https://images.forbes.com/forbesinsights/StudyPDFs/Innovation_Through_Diversity.pdf.

26. Díaz-García, Cristina, Angela González-Moreno, and Francisco Jose Sáez-Martínez. "Gender Diversity Within R&D Teams:

Its Impact on Radicalness of Innovation." *Innovation* 15, no. 2 (December 17, 2014): 149-60. doi:10.5172/impp.2013.15.2.149.

27. Hunt, Vivian, Dennis Layton, and Sara Prince. "Why Diversity Matters." McKinsey & Company. January 2015. https://www .mckinsey.com/business-functions/organization/our-insights/why -diversity-matters.

28. Stauffer, Brian. "Follow the Thread: The Need for Supply Chain Transparency in the Garment and Footwear Industry." Human Rights Watch. June 6, 2017. https://www.hrw.org/report/2017/04 /20/follow-thread/need-supply-chain-transparency-garment-and -footwear-industry#_ftn2.

29. Doherty, Mike. "The Story Behind the Stuff: Consumers' Growing Interest in 'Real' Products." *Fast Company*. October 18, 2012. https://www.fastcompany.com/3002249/story-behind -stuff-consumers-growing-interest-real-products.

30. Paul, Eve Turow. "Beyond Kimchi and Kale: How Millennial 'Foodies' Are Challenging the Supply Chain from Farm to Table." *Forbes*. November 11, 2016. https://www.forbes.com/sites /eveturowpaul/2016/11/11/how-foodies-are-slowly-upending-the -ag-supply-chain/#1c4f46751421.

31. Joyce, Lori. "About." Betterwith Ice Cream. Accessed January 16, 2018. http://betterwith.com/about/.

32. "B.C. Entrepreneur Introduces First Brand of Traceable Ice Cream." *Progressive Dairyman: Canada*. March 8, 2017. https:// www.progressivedairycanada.com/topics/people/b-c-entrepreneur -introduces-first-brand-of-traceable-ice-cream.

33. Gill, Alexandra. "Cupcake Entrepreneur Launches Ethical, High-Fat Ice Cream Brand." *Globe and Mail*. April 10, 2017. https:// www.theglobeandmail.com/report-on-business/small-business /sb-growth/cupcake-retailer-launches-new-brand-of-traceable-ice -cream/article33474210/.

34. Colman, Tyler. "Drink Outside the Box." *New York Times*. August 17, 2008. http://www.nytimes.com/2008/08/18/opinion /18colman.html.

CHAPTER 3

1. Allen, James, James Root, and Andrew Schwedel. "The Firm of the Future." Bain & Company. April 12, 2017. http://www.bain .com/publications/articles/firm-of-the-future.aspx.

2. Robischon, Noah. "Neil Blumenthal and Danny Meyer on the State of Customer Service." *Fast Company*. January 9, 2017. https://www.fastcompany.com/3066372/neil-blumenthal-and -danny-meyer-on-the-state-of-customer-service.

3. "Why a Salad Company Has a Tech Team." Medium. January 20, 2016. https://medium.com/sweetgreen/why-a-salad-company-has -a-tech-team-71c131f9aad2.

4. Rapkin, Mickey. "The Founders of Sweetgreen Are Building a Farm-to-Counter Empire, One Bowl at a Time." *Fast Company*.

November 21, 2016. https://www.fastcompany.com/3065372
/the-founders-of-sweetgreen-are-building-a-farm-to-counter
-empire-o.
5. O'Shea, Dan. "ThirdLove Releases Fit Finder 2.0 to Refine Bra-
Fitting." Retail Dive. June 20, 2017. https://www.retaildive
.com/news/thirdlove-releases-fit-finder-20-to-refine-bra-fitting
/445435/.
6. Harlow, Poppy, and Rebecca Minkoff. Comment on "Rebecca
Minkoff: The Millennial Designer." *Boss Files with Poppy Harlow*
(podcast). May 15, 2017. https://itunes.apple.com/us/podcast/boss
-files-with-poppy-harlow/id1201282406?mt=2.
7. Morgan, Jacob. "Staying Human in a Technology-Obsessed
World." *The Future Organization* (audio blog). April 13, 2017.
https://thefutureorganization.com/staying-human-technology
-obsessed-world/.
8. Morgan. "Staying Human."

CHAPTER 4

1. Keith, Elise. "55 Million: A Fresh Look at the Number,
Effectiveness, and Cost of Meetings in the U.S." Lucid Meetings
Blog. December 4, 2015. https://blog.lucidmeetings.com/blog
/fresh-look-number-effectiveness-cost-meetings-in-us.
2. Baer, Drake. "$37 Billion Is Lost Every Year on These 12
Meeting Mistakes." Business Insider. April 9, 2014. http://
www.businessinsider.com/37-billion-is-lost-every-year-on-these
-meeting-mistakes-2014-4.
3. Perlow, Leslie A., Constance Noonan Hadley, and Eunice Eun.
"Stop the Meeting Madness." *Harvard Business Review*. June 26,
2017. https://hbr.org/2017/07/stop-the-meeting-madness.
4. Keith. "Cost of Meetings in the U.S."
5. Vanderkam, Laura. "Will Half of People Be Working Remotely
by 2020?" *Fast Company*. August 14, 2014. https://www
.fastcompany.com/3034286/will-half-of-people-be-working
-remotely-by-2020.
6. Rai, Karan. "We Have It Backwards: It's Time to Start Making
a Purpose Case for Business." ChiefExecutive.net. November 14,
2017. https://chiefexecutive.net/backwards-time-start-making
-purpose-case-business/.
7. Bedford, Tori. "Sherry Turkle: Reclaiming Conversation." WGBH.
October 16, 2015. https://www.wgbh.org/news/post/sherry-turkle
-reclaiming-conversation.
8. Turkle, Sherry. "Stop Googling. Let's Talk." *New York Times*.
September 26, 2015. https://www.nytimes.com/2015/09/27
/opinion/sunday/stop-googling-lets-talk.html.
9. Smith, Ned. "Distracted Workers Cost U.S. Businesses $650
Billion a Year." Business News Daily. October 5, 2010. https://
www.businessnewsdaily.com/267-distracted-workforce-costs
-businesses-billions.html.

10. Giang, Vivian. "These Are the Long-Term Effects of Multitasking." *Fast Company*. March 1, 2016. https://www.fastcompany.com /3057192/these-are-the-long-term-effects-of-multitasking.

11. McCracken, Harry. "Satya Nadella Rewrites Microsoft's Code." *Fast Company*. October 12, 2017. https://www.fastcompany.com /40457458/satya-nadella-rewrites-microsofts-code.

12. Morgan, Jacob. "Ep 71: Rethinking Our Personal and Professional Relationships." *The Future of Work Podcast with Jacob Morgan* (podcast). Accessed February 1, 2018. https://player.fm/series/the -future-of-work-podcast-with-jacob-morgan-futurist-workplace -careers-employee-experience-engagement/ep-71-rethinking-our -personal-and-professional-relationships.

13. Chopovsky, Max. "Design Your Office to Fulfill Employees' Most Basic Needs." Entrepreneur.com. Accessed January 15, 2018. https://www.entrepreneur.com/article/247698.

14. *How Brainwriting Can Neutralize the Loudmouths*. Produced by Leigh Thompson. Performed by Leigh Thompson. Kellogg (Northwestern). Accessed January 23, 2018. http://www .kellogg.northwestern.edu/news_articles/2014/06262014-video -thompson-brainwriting.aspx.

15. Cain, Susan. "How to Talk in Meetings When You Hate Talking in Meetings." Interview by Dana Rousmaniere. *Harvard Business Review*. April 21, 2016. https://hbr.org/2016/04/how-to-talk-in -meetings-when-you-hate-talking-in-meetings.

16. Weiner, Jeff. "Managing Compassionately." LinkedIn. October 15, 2012. https://www.linkedin.com/pulse/20121015034012 -22330283-managing-compassionately/.

17. Snyder, Bill. "Jeff Weiner: Manage Compassionately, and Prepare for the Next Worker Revolution." Stanford Graduate School of Business. February 24, 2017. https://www.gsb.stanford .edu/insights/jeff-weiner-manage-compassionately-prepare-next -worker-revolution.

18. Anderson, L.V. "Spectacular Advice." Slate. March 2, 2016. http://www.slate.com/articles/business/the_ladder/2016/03/career _and_productivity_advice_from_warby_parker_co_founder_and _co_ceo_dave.html.

CHAPTER 5

1. Franco, G. "Ramazzini and Workers' Health." *The Lancet* 354, no. 9181 (September 4, 1999): 858–61. doi:10.1016/s0140-6736 (99)80042-7.

2. Ramazzini, Bernardino. "De Morbis Artificum Diatriba [Diseases of Workers]." Edited by Elizabeth Fee, PhD, and Theodore M. Brown, PhD. *American Journal of Public Health* 91, no. 9 (September 1, 2001): 1380–82. http://ajph.aphapublications.org/doi /pdf/10.2105/AJPH.91.9.1382.

3. Valet, Vicky. "More Than Two-Thirds of U.S. Employers Currently Offer Wellness Programs, Study Says." *Forbes*. July 8,

2015.   https://www.forbes.com/sites/vickyvalet/2015/07/08/more
-than-two-thirds-of-u-s-employers-currently-offer-wellness
-programs-study-says/#35b5f7e5231d.

4. Fry, Erika. "Corporate Wellness Programs: Healthy or Hokey?"
Fortune.   March   15,   2017.   http://fortune.com/2017/03/15
/corporate-health-wellness-programs/.

5. Berry, Leonard L., Ann M. Mirabito, and William B. Baun.
"What's the Hard Return on Employee Wellness Programs?"
Harvard Business Review. July 31, 2014. https://hbr.org/2010/12
/whats-the-hard-return-on-employee-wellness-programs.

6. *Exploring the Value Proposition for Workforce Health.* Report.
February   2015.   https://www.shrm.org/ResourcesAndTools
/hr-topics/benefits/Documents/HPP-Business-Leader-Survey-Full
-Report_FINAL.pdf.

7. Berry et al. "What's the Hard Return."

8. Kohll, Alan. "The Top Corporate Wellness Trends to Watch for
in 2017." *Forbes.* January 18, 2017. https://www.forbes.com
/sites/alankohll/2017/01/18/the-top-corporate-wellness-trends-to
-watch-for-in-2017/#1b1c85157b28

9. Porter, Jane. "Enough with the Ping-Pong Tables—Creative Perks
That People Actually Care About." *Fast Company.* August 1,
2014.   https://www.fastcompany.com/3033795/enough-with-the
-ping-pong-tables-creative-perks-that-people-actually-care.

10. "Healthy Culture." Vynamic. Accessed January 25, 2018. https://
vynamic.com/healthy-culture/.

11. O'Donnell, Lilly. "What Happens When You Ditch After-hours
Email?" OpenWork. January 12, 2017. http://www.openwork.org
/healthcare-management-consulting/.

12. Batchelor, Charles. " 'Up or Out' Is Part of Industry Culture."
Financial Times. April 20, 2011. https://www.ft.com/content
/d42434b2-6b69-11e0-a53e-00144feab49a.

13. Great Place to Work Institute. "Vynamic." Accessed November
15, 2017. http://reviews.greatplacetowork.com/vynamic.

14. Butcher, Dan. "You Have a 4% Chance of Getting a Job at
Deloitte. This Is What It Takes." EFinancialCareers. March 15,
2016.   https://news.efinancialcareers.com/us-en/239038/getting
-a-job-at-deloitte/.

15. Riordan, Christine M. "We All Need Friends at Work." *Harvard
Business Review.* July 3, 2013. https://hbr.org/2013/07/we-all
-need-friends-at-work.

16. "Vynamic." Great Place to Work Reviews. Accessed January 26,
2018. http://reviews.greatplacetowork.com/vynamic.

17. Rothfeld, Lindsay. "7 Companies with Amazingly Unique Wellness
Programs." Mashable. May 15, 2015. http://mashable.com/2015
/05/15/unique-corporate-wellness-programs/#pBktSh9B7Eqg.

18. Fisher, Jen. "A Better Bottom Line." Work Well Podcast. Podcast
audio, May 7, 2018. https://www2.deloitte.com/us/en/pages/about
-deloitte/articles/workwell-podcast-series-one.html.

19. "Vynamic." *Fortune*. October 17, 2017. http://fortune.com/best -medium-workplaces/vynamic-35/.
20. "COPE Health Solutions Career Overview." Glassdoor. Accessed January 26, 2018. https://www.glassdoor.com/Overview/Working -at-COPE-Health-Solutions-EI_IE290160.11,32.htm.
21. "UDG Healthcare Announces the Acquisition of US-based Healthcare Consultancy Firm for Up to $32m." UDG Healthcare. July 12, 2017. https://www.udghealthcare.com/media/press -releases/udg-healthcare-announces-the-acquisition-of-us-based -healthcare-consultancy-firm-for-up-to-32m.
22. "Surgeon General: Most Common Disease Is Isolation." "Matter of Fact with Soledad O'Brien." June 18, 2016. http://matteroffact .tv/surgeon-general-common-disease-isolation/.
23. Porath, Christine. "No Time to Be Nice at Work." *New York Times*. June 19, 2015. https://www.nytimes.com/2015/06/21 /opinion/sunday/is-your-boss-mean.html.
24. Slopen, Natalie, Robert J. Glynn, Julie E. Buring, Tené T. Lewis, David R. Williams, and Michelle A. Albert. "Job Strain, Job Insecurity, and Incident Cardiovascular Disease in the Women's Health Study: Results from a 10-Year Prospective Study." *Public Library of Science* 7, no. 7 (July 18, 2012). doi:10.1371/journal .pone.0040512.
25. Riskin, Arieh, Amir Erez, Trevor A. Foulk, Amir Kugelman, Ayala Gover, Irit Shoris, Kinneret S. Riskin, and Peter A. Bamberger. "The Impact of Rudeness on Medical Team Performance: A Randomized Trial." *Pediatrics*. August 10, 2015. http://pediatrics .aappublications.org/content/early/2015/08/05/peds.2015 -1385.
26. "The Well Building Standard." International Well Building Institute. Accessed February 26, 2018. https://www.wellcertified .com/en/explore-standard.

CHAPTER 6

1. Staff, Inc. "The 50 Best Places to Work in 2016." Inc.com. June 2016. https://www.inc.com/magazine/201606/inc-staff/best-work places-2016.html.
2. Sullivan, Paul. "Firms Learn That as They Help Charities, They Also Help Their Brands." *New York Times*. November 6, 2017. https://www.nytimes.com/2017/11/06/business/corporate -philanthropy.html.
3. Lee, Jan. "How Stakeholder Engagement Boosts Brand and Brand Values." *Corporate Responsibility Magazine*. July 12, 2017. http:// thecro.com/corporate-reputation/how-stakeholder-engagement -boosts-brand-and-brand-values/.
4. Garton, Eric, and Michael Mankins. "Engaging Your Employees Is Good, but Don't Stop There." *Harvard Business Review*. December 9, 2015. https://hbr.org/2015/12/engaging-your -employees-is-good-but-dont-stop-there.

5. Black, Renata M. "Brian Berger: The Apple of Underwear." *Huffington Post*. April 7, 2016. https://www.huffingtonpost.com /renata-m-black/brian-berger--the-apple-o_b_9636580.html.
6. "New York's Fastest-Growing Companies." Crain's. Accessed February 1, 2018. http://www.crainsnewyork.com/features/2017 -fast50/mack-weldon.
7. "Mack Weldon CEO, Brian Berger." Telephone interview by author. 2017.
8. Ellis, Laura. "Loop Them In: How to Help Your Remote Employees Feel like Local Volunteers." VolunteerMatch. April 17, 2014. https://blogs.volunteermatch.org/volunteeringiscsr/2014/04 /17/loop-them-in-how-to-help-your-remote-employees-feel-like -local-volunteers/.
9. Sullivan, Paul. "Firms Learn That as They Help Charities, They Also Help Their Brands." *New York Times*. November 6, 2017. https://www.nytimes.com/2017/11/06/business/corporate -philanthropy.html.

CHAPTER 7

1. "Bored . . . and Brilliant? A Challenge to Disconnect from Your Phone." NPR. January 12, 2015. https://www.npr.org/sections /alltechconsidered/2015/01/12/376717870/bored-and-brilliant -a-challenge-to-disconnect-from-your-phone.
2. Segran, Elizabeth. "What Really Happens to Your Brain and Body During a Digital Detox." *Fast Company*. July 30, 2015. https://www.fastcompany.com/3049138/what-really-happens-to -your-brain-and-body-during-a-digital-detox.
3. Segran. "Digital Detox."
4. Richtel, Matt. "Digital Devices Deprive Brain of Needed Downtime." *New York Times*. August 24, 2010. http://www .nytimes.com/2010/08/25/technology/25brain.html.
5. Mele, Christopher. "Coffee Shops Skip Wi-Fi to Encourage Customers to Actually Talk." *New York Times*. May 09, 2017. https://www.nytimes.com/2017/05/09/technology/coffee-shop -wifi-access.html.
6. U.S. Department of Labor. *Employee Benefits in the United States–March 2017*. Report. July 21, 2017. https://www.bls.gov /news.release/pdf/ebs2.pdf.
7. "Glassdoor Survey Finds Americans Forfeit Half of Their Earned Vacation/Paid Time Off." Glassdoor. May 24, 2017. https://www .glassdoor.com/press/glassdoor-survey-finds-americans-forfeit -earned-vacationpaid-time/.
8. Huppke, Rex. "Bosses Must Become Vacation Evangelists." *Chicago Tribune*. May 19, 2017. http://www.chicagotribune.com /business/careers/ijustworkhere/ct-need-for-vacations-huppke-work -advice-0521-biz-20170518-column.html.
9. Schwartz, Tony, and Christine Porath. "Your Boss's Work-Life Balance Matters as Much as Your Own." *Harvard Business*

Review. July 10, 2014. https://hbr.org/2014/07/your-bosss-work -life-balance-matters-as-much-as-your-own.

10. Huppke. "Bosses Must Become Vacation Evangelists."

11. Delvv. "Sex or Smartphone? 29% of Americans Choose Their Device." PR Newswire. August 9, 2016. https://www.prnewswire .com/news-releases/sex-or-smartphone-29-of-americans-choose -their-device-300310831.html.

12. Deloitte. *2017 Global Mobile Consumer Survey: US Edition.* Report. Accessed February 6, 2018. https://www2.deloitte .com/content/dam/Deloitte/us/Documents/technology-media -telecommunications/us-tmt-2017-global-mobile-consumer -survey-executive-summary.pdf.

13. "Walker & Company Brands." Crunchbase. Accessed February 06, 2018. https://www.crunchbase.com/organization/walker -company-brands.

14. McCorvey, J. J. "Tristan Walker's Challenge: 'How Can I Be the Best CEO I Can Be?'" *Entrepreneur.* July 5, 2017. https://www .entrepreneur.com/article/296088.

15. Blanda, Sean. "Bevel's Tristan Walker: The Best Ideas Are Brewed Out of Authenticity." Sean Blanda. June 11, 2015. http:// seanblanda.com/bevels-tristan-walker-the-best-ideas-are-brewed -out-of-authenticity/.

16. Smith, Benson, and Tony Rutigliano. "The Truth About Turnover." Gallup. February 4, 2002. http://news.gallup.com /businessjournal/316/truth-about-turnover.aspx.

17. Malcolm, Hadley. "REI Closing on Black Friday for 1st Time in Push to #OptOutside." *USA Today.* October 26, 2015. https:// www.usatoday.com/story/money/2015/10/26/rei-closing-on-black -friday-for-first-time-in-its-history/74627872/.

18. Chung, Frank. "Why PepsiCo CEO Asks His Team to 'Leave Loudly.'" *The Daily Telegraph.* September 12, 2017. https://www .dailytelegraph.com.au/business/work/why-pepsico-ceo-asks-his -team-to-leave-loudly/news-story/5467b3ffff387c3a5dd79ac3a2 45c868.

19. Lorang, Bart. "Paid Vacation? Not Cool. You Know What's Cool? Paid, PAID Vacation." FullContact. July 10, 2012. https://www .fullcontact.com/blog/paid-paid-vacation/.

20. Weller, Chris. "A CEO Who Gives His Employees $2,000 to Go on Vacation Says People Are More Productive than Ever." Business Insider. September 26, 2016. http://www.businessinsider.com/ceo -pays-employees-2000-to-go-on-vacation-2016-9.

CHAPTER 8

1. "The Privacy Crisis: Taking a Toll on Employee Engagement." Steelcase. December 15, 2017. https://www.steelcase.com/research /articles/privacy-crisis/.

2. Hyder, Shama. "The Future of Workplace Design: The FETCH Model." *Forbes.* November 16, 2017. https://www.forbes.com

/sites/shamahyder/2017/11/16/the-future-of-workplace-design-the
-fetch-model/.

3. Zimmerman, Kaytie. "Can Having a Best Friend at Work Make
You More Productive?" *Forbes*. December 5, 2016. https://www
.forbes.com/sites/kaytiezimmerman/2016/12/05/can-having
-a-best-friend-at-work-make-you-more-productive/.

4. Miller, Meg. "Squarespace's New Offices Are Very Serious."
Co.Design. September 29, 2016. https://www.fastcodesign.com
/3064163/squarespaces-new-offices-are-very-serious.

5. "Career-Launching Companies List." Wealthfront. Accessed
February 26, 2018. https://blog.wealthfront.com/wp-content
/uploads/2017/10/2018_Career-Launching_List-10.pdf.

6. Patel, Mehul. "2017 Global Brand Health Report." Hired.
October 26, 2017. https://hired.com/blog/highlights/hired-brand
-health-report-2017/.

7. "100 Best Workplaces for Millennials." *Fortune*. Accessed February
26, 2018. http://fortune.com/best-workplaces-millennials/2015/.

8. Miller. "Squarespace's New Offices."

9. Leadem, Rose. "What We Learned from Touring Squarespace's
Gorgeous New Headquarters." *Entrepreneur*. October 21, 2016.
https://www.entrepreneur.com/article/284017.

10. Fries, Laura. "Inspirational Office Design: A Way to Retain
Millennials." *Business Journals*. May 3, 2017. https://www
-bizjournals-com.cdn.ampproject.org/c/s/www.bizjournals.com
/bizjournals/how-to/growth-strategies/2017/05/inspirational-office
-design-a-way-to-retain.amp.html.

11. Hill, Adrienne, and Jana Kasperkevic. "Do Open-Space Offices
Really Make Us More Productive?" WBFO *All Things Considered*.
June 19, 2017. http://news.wbfo.org/post/do-open-space-offices
-really-make-us-more-productive.

12. Miller, Rex, Mabel Casey, and Mark Konchar. "Chapter 10:
They Did It, You Can Too." In *Change Your Space, Change Your
Culture: How Engaging Workspaces Lead to Transformation and
Growth*, 168. New York: Wiley, 2014.

13. Miller, Casey, and Konchar. *Change Your Space*. 169.

14. Miller, Casey, and Konchar. *Change Your Space*. 168.

15. Miller, Casey, and Konchar. *Change Your Space*. 170.

16. Miller, Casey, and Konchar. *Change Your Space*. 171.

17. Kirk, Patricia. "Exclusive Q&A: CBRE's Lew Horne on Next-Gen
Creative Space." Bisnow. November 9, 2015. https://www.bisnow
.com/los-angeles/news/office/exclusive-qa-with-cbres-socal-leader
-lew-horne-on-next-gen-creative-space-52117.

18. Kirk. " Next-Gen Creative Space."

19. Lee, Kyungjoon, John S. Brownstein, Richard G. Mills, Isaac
S. Kohane. "Close Proximity Leads to Better Science." PLoS
ONE, December 15, 2010. https://doi.org/10.1371/journal.pone
.0014279.

CHAPTER 9

1. Beer, Michael, Magnus Finnström, and Derek Schrader. "Why Leadership Training Fails—and What to Do About It." *Harvard Business Review.* October 9, 2016. https://hbr.org/2016/10/why -leadership-training-fails-and-what-to-do-about-it.
2. Miller, Adam. "3 Things Millennials Want in a Career (Hint: It's Not More Money)." *Fortune.* March 26, 2015. http://fortune.com /2015/03/26/3-things-millennials-want-in-a-career-hint-its-not -more-money/.
3. "The Most Popular Courses of 2016." Coursera Blog. January 3, 2017. https://blog.coursera.org/popular-courses-2016/.
4. Elejalde-Ruiz, Alexia. "Career Development Is Top Priority for Employers Seeking to Retain Talent." *Chicago Tribune.* March 29, 2016. http://www.chicagotribune.com/business/careers/ct -career-development-perk-0330-biz-20160329-story.html.
5. Weaver, Stephanie. "Why Employees with a Side Hustle Are Better at Their Jobs." *Inc.* July 10, 2011. https://www.inc.com/stephanie -weaver/why-employees-with-a-side-hustle-are-better-at-the.html.
6. "2017 Annual Workplace Survey." Addison Group. May 2017. http://www.addisongroup.com/_media/files/downloads/Addison _Group_2017_Workplace_Survey_Full_Results.pdf.
7. Boushey, Heather, and Sarah Jane Glynn. "There Are Significant Business Costs to Replacing Employees." Center for American Progress. November 16, 2012. https://www.americanprogress.org /wp-content/uploads/2012/11/CostofTurnover.pdf.
8. Human Resources Podcasts North. "Workplace Loyalties Change, but the Value of Mentoring Doesn't." Knowledge@Wharton. May 16, 2007. http://knowledge.wharton.upenn.edu/article/workplace -loyalties-change-but-the-value-of-mentoring-doesnt/.
9. Stein, Jon. "How We've Built the Betterment Way." Betterment. Accessed February 9, 2018. https://s3.amazonaws.com/betterment -prod-cdn/documents/The_Betterment_Way_2017_08_17.pdf.
10. "About." Meet Refinery29. Accessed February 23, 2018. https:// corporate.r29.com/about#about-intro.

CHAPTER 10

1. "Giving Thanks Can Make You Happier." Harvard Health Publishing. Accessed February 9, 2018. https://www.health .harvard.edu/healthbeat/giving-thanks-can-make-you-happier.
2. Settembre, Jeanette. "SoulCycle CEO Tells Moneyish How It Gained Its Cult-Like Following, Compares the Fitness Brand to Disney." Moneyish. November 10, 2017. https://moneyish.com /ish/soulcycle-ceo-tells-moneyish-how-it-gained-its-cult-like -following-compares-the-fitness-brand-to-disney/.
3. Yohn, Denise Lee. "SoulCycle Uses a Freedom Within a Framework Approach to Flourish." *Forbes.* November 30, 2016. https://www.forbes.com/sites/deniselyohn/2016/11/30/soulcycle -uses-a-freedom-within-a-framework-approach-to-flourish/.

4. "Meet RUDY VOLCY, the Most Decorated Rockstar at SOUL HQ." SoulCycle. August 9, 2016. https://www.soul-cycle.com /community/inside/meet-rudy-volcy-the-most-decorated-rockstar -at-soul-hq/2237/.

5. "Meet RUDY VOLCY."

6. Ringen, Jonathan. "SoulCycle Wants You to Join Its Tribe." *Fast Company*. August 8, 2016. https://www.fastcompany.com /3062190/soulcycle-wants-you-to-join-its-tribe.

7. "Item 10: I Have a Best Friend at Work." Gallup. May 26, 1999. http://news.gallup.com/businessjournal/511/item-10-best-friend -work.aspx.

8. Gulliford, Liz, et al. "Recent Work on the Concept of Gratitude in Philosophy and Psychology." *Journal of Value Inquiry* 47, no. 3 (September 2013): 285–317. doi.org/10.1007/s10790-013-9387-8.

9. Seppala, Emma, and Kim Cameron. "Proof That Positive Work Cultures Are More Productive." *Harvard Business Review*. December 1, 2015. https://hbr.org/2015/12/proof-that-positive-work -cultures-are-more-productive.

10. Simon-Thomas, Emiliana R., and Jeremy Adam Smith. "How Grateful Are Americans?" *Greater Good*. January 10, 2013. https://greatergood.berkeley.edu/article/item/how_grateful_are _americans.

11. Derek Irvine and Eric Mosley. *The Power of Thanks: How Social Recognition Empowers Employees and Creates a Best Place to Work*. McGraw-Hill, 2015, xvi.

INDEX

ABOUT THE AUTHOR

Erica Keswin is an expert in the business of relationships who helps top-of-the-class businesses, organizations, and individuals improve their performance through honoring relationships, always with an eye toward high-tech for human touch. She is a passionate dot-connector in her speaking, workshops, writing, consulting, research, and personal life.

Erica has worked for over 20 years in organization and leadership development. She was a consultant at the Hay Group and Booz Allen Hamilton, Inc., and worked as an Executive Director at Russell Reynolds Associates. She also served as an Executive Coach at New York University's Stern School of Business.

Erica contributes regularly to *Forbes*, the *Harvard Business Review*, *Entrepreneur*, and *Quartz at Work*. She is an active keynote speaker on organizational culture who has recently spoken at Propelify Innovation Festival, Virtuoso Global Forum, the New York Times, Girl's Lounge at SXSW and WorkHuman.

In addition to being an author and sought-after speaker, Erica is the founder of the Spaghetti Project, a platform devoted to sharing the science and stories of human connections with global brands, community groups, teams, and individuals. Inspired by a 2015 Cornell study showing that firemen who eat together are better at their jobs (they save more lives!), this platform is a hats-off to the firemen and their go-to firehouse meals.

Erica received her MBA from the Kellogg Graduate School of Management at Northwestern University, and her BA from the University of Vermont. She sits on the Advisory Board of DoSomething Strategic, the strategy arm of DoSomething.org.

She lives on the Upper West Side of Manhattan with her husband, Jeff, their three children, and their dog, Cruiser.